The British Sailor

Overleaf. Women helping to entertain sailors in port, early nineteenth century.

The British Sailor

Richard Garrett

"No man will be a sailor who has contrivance enough to get himself into a jail; for being in a ship is being in jail, with the chance of being drowned."
(Samuel Johnson)

WAYLAND PUBLISHERS LONDON

ALSO IN THE ENGLISH LIFE SERIES

English Life in Chaucer's Day
English Life in Tudor Times
English Life in the Seventeenth Century
English Life in the Eighteenth Century
English Life in the Nineteenth Century
The English Servant
Roger Hart

The Edwardians
English Life in the First World War
Christopher Martin

English Life between the World Wars
Marion Yass

The Search for Prosperity: Emigration from Britain 1815–1939
Richard Garrett

The Cost of Living in Britain
Leith McGrandle

Strangers to England: Immigration to England 1100–1945
Colin Nicolson

The British Soldier
Matthew Holden

Crime and Punishment in Britain
John Tobias

First published 1974 by
Wayland (Publishers) Ltd
101 Gray's Inn Road London WC1

ISBN 85340 402 X

Filmset by Keyspools Ltd, Golborne, Lancs
Printed in Great Britain by
Tinling (1973) Ltd, Prescot, Merseyside

Contents

1 *Prelude*

Three months before the defeat of the Armada in July, 1588, the Venetian ambassador in Madrid had warned the Spanish monarch about the perils of pitting his men and ships against English sailors. They had, he wrote, "a name above all in the West for being expert and enterprising in all maritime affairs, and the finest fighters upon the sea."

"The English," he explained, "never yield, and although they be put to flight, and broken, they ever return, athirst for revenge, to renew the attack, so long as they have a breath of life."

King Philip II's reply is not recorded – though the ambassador's views did not cause him to modify his plans for invasion. Possibly he disagreed with them. If this was the case, the events of a few days later should have taught him a salutory lesson. Without any loss to his own ships, Sir Francis Drake sailed into the harbour at Cadiz, and put thirty-four Spanish ships to the torch. Before returning home, he extended his voyage to include the Azores, where he captured a £114,000 prize named the *San Felipe*. He had, as he told Queen Elizabeth I, "singed the King of Spain's beard." The monarch was delighted – especially as her own share of the booty amounted to £40,000.

But there had been other events, elsewhere in the world, which should have counselled King Philip to be cautious. English privateers had caused serious losses to Spanish shipping in the Caribbean; and – with considerable rewards to himself, his sailors, his sponsors and his sovereign – Drake had made short shrift of treasure-laden Spanish vessels off the west coast of South America.

So many failures should have encouraged Philip to heed the ambassador's opinions, but long established ideas take an equally long time to die. It was only, he may have reflected, comparatively recently that England had shown any pretentions of becoming a maritime power. Venice had been, and still was, the capital of world shipping. Until Richard Hakluyt wrote his *Principall Navigations, Voyages, Traffics and Discoveries of the English Nation* in 1589, the only works on navigation were those published in Spain and Italy. The discovery of North and South America: the notion of rounding southern Africa to reach the rich lands of India, Cathay (China) and the Spice Islands – all these had been the achievements of Portuguese and Spanish mariners.

Admittedly, in 1497, John Cabot had sailed across the Atlantic at the behest of Henry VII. Seeking an alternative route to the Far East, he dis-

King Philip II of Spain spent many years trying to stop the daring exploits of such English sailors as Hawkins and Drake, but without success.

Opposite. English reinforcements on the way to France during the Hundred Years' War

Above. John Cabot, commissioned by Henry VII of England to find the north-west passage to Asia, sailed the Atlantic in 1497 – and landed in Canada.

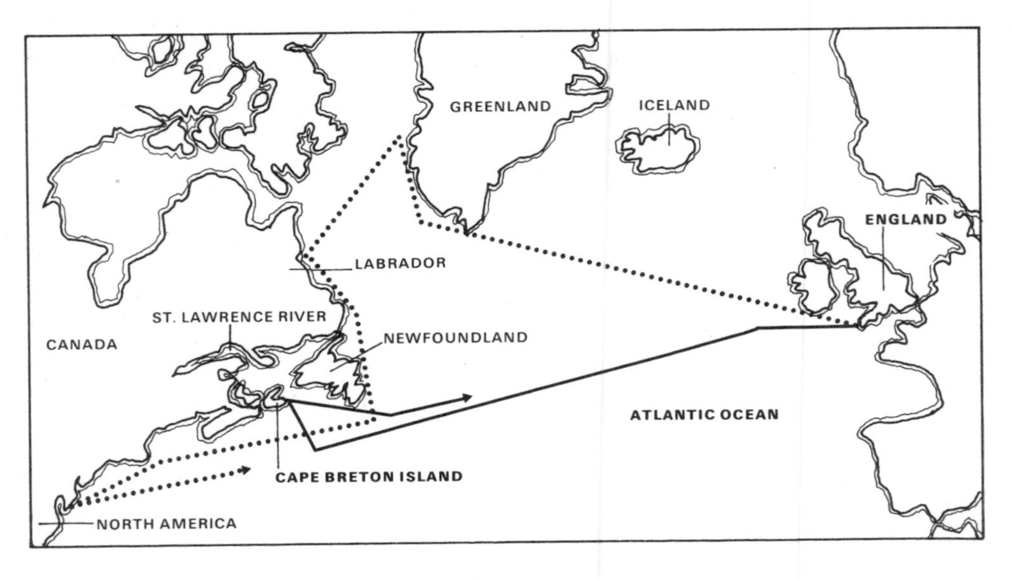

Above right. Map showing Cabot's two voyages across the Atlantic to the north coast of America.

covered Newfoundland (which he wrongly thought to be the edge of Asia) and sailed along the coast of Labrador.* But, like Christopher Columbus, Cabot had been born in Genoa. It was not until the coming of Hawkins and Drake, that English-bred mariners showed any great talent for long range exploration. Hitherto, the voyages of British sailors had been mostly confined to the coastal trade, and journeys across the Channel and the North Sea.

Nor had British shipping amounted to much. In the fourteenth century, Richard II (1367–1400) had passed the first navigation laws with the idea of ensuring that only English vessels should carry freight to English ports. The measures turned out to be completely impracticable – for the simple reason that the nation did not possess sufficient ships. Two centuries later, Sir Walter Raleigh was bemoaning the fact that, whilst there did not seem to be a single tree in Holland, that country was producing much better vessels than Britain – and many more of them. Their design enabled them to be manned by only one-third of the crew carried by an English merchantman, and a thousand ships a year were being built.

"The situation of England," he wrote, "lieth far better for a storehouse to serve the South West and North East Kingdoms than theirs do, and we have the far better means to do it if we apply ourselves to do it." He noted that, whilst English merchants were sending only one hundred vessels a year to trade with the Elbe, Königsberg, and Danzig, businessmen in the Low Countries were dispatching three thousand. "The Hollanders send into France, Spain, Portugal and Italy from the East Kingdoms, passing through the Sound [the Straits of Dover, presumably], with Baltic produce, about two thousand merchant ships, and we have none in that course . . . the Dutch trade to every port and town in France, and we only to five or six!!"

For an island race, which was later to become renowned for the exploits of her sailors, England was strangely slow to realise the necessity for well-equipped vessels manned by able crews. Until Richard I

* Cabot was the first mariner to keep a log, recording the events and progress of his voyage.

Richard II wanted England to be a naval power, but did not have the ships to achieve his aim.

travelled through the Mediterranean on his way to the Crusades in 1189, the former resembled abbreviated versions of the Viking longships, propelled through the water by a mixture of oars and sails. The rowers, unlike enslaved Mediterranean oarsmen, were free men: their efforts, as they sweated away, were accompanied by the first sea shanties. Later, these work-songs were composed to bring unison and effort to such strenuous jobs as heaving on ropes, and hauling up the anchor. In some instances, the man in charge sang his instructions, whilst the sailors chorused the refrain. Life on ship was nothing if not operatic.

The Early Ships

The Normans had provided the fighting qualities of English vessels during the eleventh century, whilst Anglo Saxons were employed to sail them. Consequently, the names of what might roughly be called the naval officers (Admiral, Captain and Lieutenant) were all of Norman origin. Those of the men who worked the boat (boatswain, coxswain, lodesman – the pilot, and the very word "seaman" itself) were derived from Anglo Saxon.

When Richard I travelled to the Mediterranean, he came across a world in which ships and shipbuilding were considerably more advanced. The pacemakers were the Venetians, who were already trading with the

Looking similar to the Vikings' longships, this Norman galley was used in William the Conqueror's invasion of England in 1066.

A fourteenth-century Venetian galley, one of the ships which influenced Richard I's ideas concerning the design of British vessels.

East. The merchandise went to the Levant by sea, and was then transported overland. It was, indeed, the attacks on these caravans by the Turks which inspired the early attempts to find another route.

Richard returned to England in 1194 with many new ideas. The Mediterranean vessels, he had found, fell roughly into two types. One was the galley – a long, slim boat, powered by oars. The other consisted of sailing vessels with more chunky hulls. Known as "cogs," they had an ample capacity for cargo, though they lacked the speed and grace of the galleys. Indeed, in some cases, the hulls were only twice as long as their widths.

A feature, Richard noted, of these ships was that, when they were fitted out for war, castles were added at the fore and aft ends. They were raised platforms from which the bowmen could fire their arrows – with wooden battlements for their protection. The monarch decided they should be introduced to British vessels.

He also agreed that the British seamen should have a charter setting down their rates of pay, their conditions of service, and a scale of punishments. Known as the Laws of Oléron, they were largely the work of Eleanor of Aquitaine, but the King gave his sanction to them.

Poor Pay and Harsh Discipline

The pay was not exactly princely, and the punishments were harsh. An admiral, who was given overall command by the sovereign for a specific operation, received 10p. a day. A captain was paid 5p. a day; a master's reward was 3p.; and a mariner – 1p. As for the penalties: if a man struck an officer, his hand was either nailed to the mast, or cut off. Tarring and feathering, keel hauling and ducking, were commonplace; and anybody who committed murder was tied to his victim's corpse and thrown overboard. By contrast, the penalty for desertion was comparatively mild: a year's imprisonment.

By the thirteenth century, castles had been added fore and aft to ships for the archers in wartime. In the big ships horses were disembarked through a door in the bows – rather like a modern car ferry.

Soldiers disembarking during the Crusades. Richard I's journey to the Holy Land introduced him to the Mediterranean type of shipping, on which he was to model his own ships.

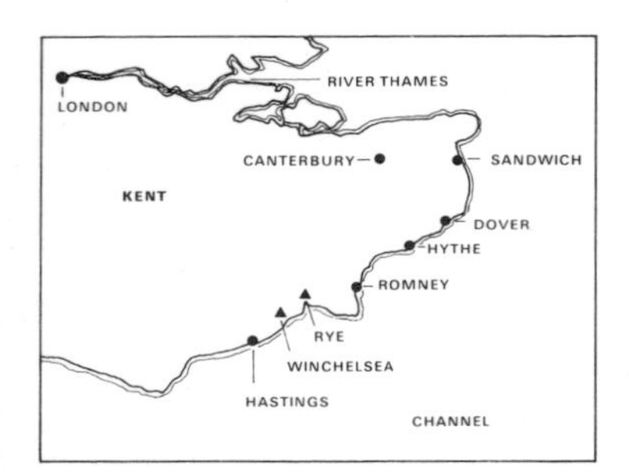

South-east England, showing the Cinque Ports of Hastings, Dover, Romney, Sandwich and Hythe. Rye and Winchelsea were included later.

Over the years, the punishments became more or less severe – according to the whim of the monarch. When King John (1167–1216) needed a navy (or thought he did), he commandeered the ships and the men. On one occasion, he instructed the East Anglian towns of Beccles, Yarmouth and Orford to provide him with two rectors (shipmasters) and 140 men. On another, he ordered all the seamen living on the Welsh coast to report for duty to Ilfracombe. Anybody who failed to turn up would, at the worst, be hanged – at the best, have all his belongings confiscated.

King John appropriated his ships and crews haphazardly. His grandson, Edward I (1239–1307), was more systematic. Doubtless reflecting on the Norman invasion, he decided that the strip of coast between Dover and Hastings was particularly vulnerable to attack from the Continent. Consequently, he made a deal with his subjects in this part of Kent and Sussex. The towns were to provide the nucleus of a navy whenever he needed it. He, in return, would grant them certain privileges. Thus, in 1277, the Cinque Ports came into being. The original five were Hastings, Romney, Hythe, Dover and Sandwich – to which, later, were added Rye and Winchelsea. Each had to supply a set number of vessels

Below. Ships of the Cinque Ports' fleet engaged in a battle with the French off Dover in 1217.

(in the case of Hastings, for example, 26 ships each manned by 21 sailors and 1 youth). The total for all the Cinque Ports was fifty-seven vessels and 1,167 sailors. The wards provided the former: the landlords supplied the crews. The recruitment of suitable men provided few problems; most of the men residing in the Cinque Ports made their living from an artful blend of fishing and piracy.

The agreement lasted until the reign of Henry VII (1457–1509), though some of the harbours had long since silted up. For instance when, in 1415, Henry V set off for Agincourt, his port of departure was Southampton. As a far distant forerunner of D-Day, the scale of the operation was impressive. All told, he mustered 1,400 vessels, carrying 6,000 men at arms, 24,000 archers, and manned – at a rough estimate – by 40,000 sailors.

Ships in Battle

In this enterprise, as in all naval operations in pre-Tudor days, there was little difference between merchantmen and warships. The king usually owned a number of vessels which, when he did not require them

On his journey to Agincourt in 1415 Henry V (*left*) used a fleet of 1,400 ships to carry his army of some 30,000 men across the Channel.

By the time Henry VII (*above*) came to the throne in 1457 some of the Cinque Ports' harbours had silted up, and were no longer of use in England's naval defences.

for warlike purposes, he chartered at a profit to merchants. Conversely, when he became involved in hostilities, he took over the merchants' ships and called back his own.

Before the temporary men-of-war went into battle, the carpenters erected the fore- and after-castles. In many ways, these appendages were like robust stage sets. Once the action was over, they were removed; and the ship became her normal, peace-loving, self again.

The crew of each vessel remained as it had been. The fighting elements were provided by the addition of an Army captain, a lieutenant, and a detachment of soldiers. Since the captain and the lieutenant both held King's commissions, and the master's authority was backed up only by Admiralty warrant, the senior military officer was in overall command of the ship. He told the master where to go; but, with no knowledge of seamanship or navigation, he had not the slightest idea of how to get there. This part of the operation was left to the shipmaster and his men.

In some ways, it reflected the social prejudices of the times. Arms were the profession of a gentleman, whilst sailing a ship was a job for a working man.

A classic example of the collaboration between soldiers and sailors is provided by the Battle of Sluys (1340), which was the first clash of arms in the Hundred Years War. One hundred and sixty-six French ships were lying at anchor in the Dutch harbour. Two hundred English vessels, their castles crammed with bowmen, sailed in to attack them. Edward III (1327–1377), who was on board one of them, is reputed to have said: "Long have I wished to meet with them, and now please God and St. George we will fight them, for much mischief they have done, and if possible I will be avenged."

Edward was, indeed, avenged – in a singularly bloody manner. According to Froissart, "This battle was very murderous and horrible. Combats at sea are more destructive than those on land, for it is not possible to escape or flee. . . . The French were completely defeated, and all the Normans and others were killed or drowned, so that not one of them escaped."

The inability "to escape or flee" was about the only major difference between a sea battle of the period and one on land. The archers manned the castles and unleashed vollies of arrows until the two fleets became close enough together for hand-to-hand combat. The object was to capture ships rather than sink them, and this type of naval engagement continued until the coming of the gun.

Officially, having taken the soldiers to the scene of conflict, the sailors' responsibility was over. They could, if they wished, become interested onlookers. In practice, however, everything suggests that, when two vessels were locked together with grappling chains, they joined in with enthusiasm.

Bows, arrows and swords were by no means the only weapons used in these early naval engagements. Indeed, a good deal of ingenuity was used in devising measures calculated to strike terror into the hearts of the enemy. One, very effective, substance was known as "Greek Fire." It was compounded of pitch, sulphur and other ingredients; and, when it was exposed to the air, it ignited. With the wind behind it, it enabled the

Fifteenth-century warships. In wartime they were commanded by soldiers and soldiers fought the sea battles. The sailor's job was to transport the soldiers to and from battle.

By the time Edward III came to the throne in 1327 a code for the welfare and punishment of sailors had been established. Discipline was severe and a man could be punished by having his hand nailed to the mast.

attackers to pour a stream of fire on to their victim's ship. The sails and rigging erupted in sheets of flame. Only vinegar, sand or earth were capable of quenching the havoc. Water had no effect upon it whatsoever.

As the two vessels came together, men at the masthead of the attacker lobbed large stones and pieces of iron down on to the other vessel's deck. And, as the soldiers boarded her, their first task was an attempt to sever the halyards and stays, and to cut down the mast. As the sails fell on to the deck, the luckless ship was not merely put out of action: the sprawl of canvas had the additional advantage of, literally, smothering the opposition. Much, understandably, depended on brute force; but some of these early commanders showed a nice sense of tactics. When, for example, Hubert de Burgh set sail in 1217 against a considerably superior force of French ships led by Eustace the Monk, he brought his vessels to windward

The first important battle of the Hundred Years' War was the naval engagement fought at Sluys in 1340 (*right*). Archers fired a barrage of arrows before the hand-to-hand fighting started.

of the enemy. The force of the breeze gave greater range and impact to his archers' arrows, and enabled his men to put "Greek Fire" to excellent use. As the result of de Burgh's craftiness, the Frenchmen retreated in confusion.

When ships were in the sovereign's service, their names were modified. For example, the peaceable *Christopher of Dartmouth* became the warlike *Christopher of the Tower* when engaged on naval operations. "Of the Tower," was, in fact, the contemporary way of saying "His Majesty's Ship." As it happens, this particular vessel was an historic one. She completely changed the English technique of sea battles; for, in 1410, she became the first warship to carry guns. Her armament consisted of three cannons and a hand gun. Thereafter, the object became predominantly to sink the enemy, and a new figure appeared on the naval scene.

From the beginning, he was called the gunner, and he bridged the gap between the seamen and the soldiers. Like the latter, he provided the fighting qualities. But, since the ship was now a platform for his gun, he was required to understand how she behaved, and what orders to give the quartermaster. As Sir William Monson, who fought against the Armada, put it: "A principal thing in a gunner at sea is to be a good helmsman, and to call him at the helm to loof or bear up, to have this better level and to observe the heaving and rolling of the sea, to take his aim at the enemy."

Before the coming of this character, the *Christopher of the Tower* had three nautical (as opposed to military) officers on board. The master steered her and attended to the navigation. The boatswain (sometimes known as the "constable") was responsible for making her go – in other words, seeing to her sails and yard arms. And the carpenter carried out all the repairs, and built the fore- and after-castles in wartime.

As the importance of gunnery grew, a radical change took place in the complements of ships of war. For instance, in 1512, a vessel named the *Mary Rose* employed 251 soldiers, 120 mariners, and 20 gunners. Just over a year later, we find the *Speedwell* with a crew of 100 mariners, 64 gunners, and no soldiers.

In the latter case, only fifty of the sailors were needed to attend to her sails. The others were there to repel boarders – or to board the enemy

In early naval battles the aim was to ram an enemy ship so that the soldiers could board it and overwhelm the forces on board, thus capturing the ship.

Early sailors only had the most primitive means of navigation, and relied largely on the sun, as can be seen *left*. Once ships had guns on board, like this one, soldiers were not necessary and sea battles no longer had to be fought at such close quarters.

ships. But, then, sailors had always been able to adapt themselves to the soldier's role. Many of them were practised pirates – and most of them were experienced in defending themselves against the attacks of others.

With the exception of Cabot and until the coming of Drake and Hawkins, the voyages of British vessels and sailors were nearly always fairly short. Coal was carried to London or the Continent from Newcastle (and, since it went by ship, it was referred to as "sea coal"); herrings were exported from Yarmouth to Spain; and there were occasional voyages to Iceland. The seaman's life was hard: his rewards were not great, though he shared in the booty when a prize ship was captured (the amount was decided by the sovereign), and there were various establishments on shore for his welfare. St. Bartholomew's Hospital in London ministered to sick seafarers, and so did its namesake at Sandwich. In 1445, a seamen's hospital was set up in Bristol; and, twelve year's later, Hull followed the West Country town's example.

Meanwhile, out at sea, English sailors cursed, and sometimes fought, and frequently sang. The words of those early shanties read rather like gibberish to the modern reader. However, in his book *Shanties from the Seven Seas*, Stan Hugill has very obligingly translated one of them:

Now the Old Man gives the order for the crowd,
To get to their stations (about the mast) and make sail,
"Haul away! Hoist 'er up!" they cry,
"Hey mate, keep clear o' me!
Can't haul with you blowin' down me bleedin' neck!"
Croaked the older shellbacks.

. . . and so on. Another ditty, which would seem to defy translation, goes:

Caupon, caupona, caupon, caupona.
Caupon hola, caupon hola,
Caupon holt, caupon holt,
Sarabossa, sarabossa.

We have obviously a long way to go before we come across jolly jack tars wondering what to do "with the drunken sailor."

Medieval cargo ships were wide and sat low in the water to enable them to carry the maximum load. The castles fore and aft were usually only erected in war time.

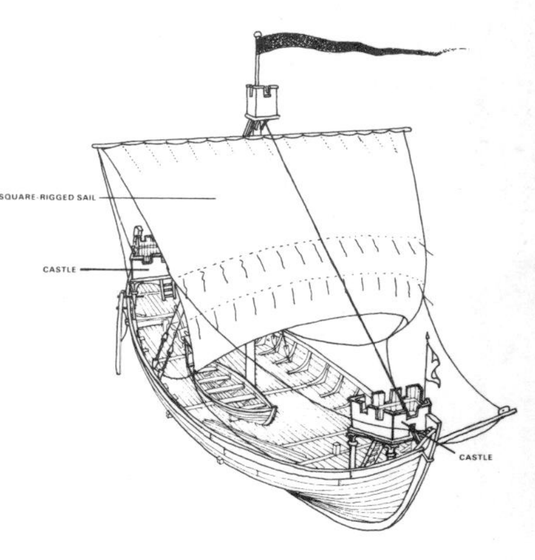

2 *The Age of Discovery*

Within a single century, the earth revealed its true form. A series of voyages, undertaken in incredibly small vessels, destroyed myths; gave the lie to land masses that were thought to have existed; and proved conclusively that the world was round. When, in 1492, Christopher Columbus suggested that the answer to the problem of finding a new route to Cathay might be to sail westwards, he was regarded as mildly eccentric. Did he not realise, the scoffers said, that the earth was flat? Travelling across the great ocean towards the setting sun could have only one result. Columbus and his small fleet would tumble off the rim into space.

The small fleet did nothing of the kind: it discovered Cuba and Haiti, and Columbus returned home to a hero's welcome. But the West Indies were not the East Indies, and the quest continued. Six years earlier, Bartholomew Diaz had been more prudent, thinking that the solution might possibly lie by way of the southern tip of Africa. During the course of his voyage, he rounded what, in view of the bad weather, he named the Cape of Storms. However, his sponsor, King John II of Portugal, was more optimistic. He believed that Diaz might well have produced a new trading route, and so he re-named it the Cape of Good Hope.

A European artist's view of Christopher Columbus discovering Cuba and Hispaniola in 1492.

In 1520, another intrepid Portuguese navigator, Ferdinand Magellan, set sail from Lisbon to prove or disprove a theory. He believed that, in the southern part of newly discovered South America, there was a channel cutting through the continent. Might this not be the break-through they were seeking? In the course of a voyage in which his fleet circumnavigated the world (but not Magellan: he died in the Philippines), he discovered a strip of water between the mainland and the island of Tierra del Fuego.

Fourteen years later, a Breton seaman named Jacques Cartier discovered the mouth of the St. Lawrence River in Canada. He might have been excused, if he had mistaken it for the entrance to a north-west passage leading to the East – a northern equivalent, as one might say, of the Magellan Strait. But no such thoughts seem to have occurred to him. He sailed back to Europe; said little about his discovery; and thirty years went by before the maps were re-drawn to include it.

Indeed, Cartier's more important contribution to the sum of seafaring knowledge was in the medical sphere. He brought back details of a mysterious sickness to which a number of his men had succumbed. Magellan's sailors had suffered from it, too, and people were beginning

Opposite. Ferdinand Magellan directing one of his crew to plumb the depths of a strange sea passage to ensure it was deep enough for his ships to sail through. It was, and the Straits of Magellan still bear his name.

A ship of the type in use during Henry VIII's reign (1508–47).

Jacques Cartier, the Breton sailor who discovered the St. Lawrence River in Canada. But probably his most important discovery was the health hazards of such long voyages, particularly scurvy.

to recognize it as yet another peril that accompanied these long voyages. It was called "scurvy."

Sir Hugh Willoughby, a distinguished soldier, conceived the idea that a north east passage might be more to the point; and, in 1553, he led an expedition in search of it. Sir Hugh's ship was wrecked on a Norwegian island, where he and his men died of scurvy. His second-in-command, a professional seaman named Richard Chancellor, was more successful. He reached Archangel, from where he travelled by sledge to Moscow as the guest of emissaries from the Tsar (Ivan the Terrible).

Sir Francis Drake

And then, in 1577, came the second circumnavigation of the world – this time by a West Country sailor who had already made several voyages to the West Indies, Francis Drake. In the hierarchy of the sea, Drake was a transitional figure. He had served his apprenticeship in a small vessel trading between the Thames estuary and the Channel ports. Writing in 1706, Ned Ward observed that the average ship master was "a seaman every bit of him, and can no more live any while on dry land than a lobster, and but for that he is obliged sometimes to make a step ashore to

A sixteenth-century ship leaving harbour. Sir Francis Drake's *Golden Hinde* probably looked rather like this, although no known authentic picture exists of this famous vessel.

new-rigg and lay in a cargo of fresh peck and tipple, he cares not tho' he never see it. . . . His very conversation is so salt that he cannot have a tooth drawn ashore without carrying his interpreter."

Drake conformed with this description in nearly every respect. He was a magnificent seaman, whose expertise at navigation was a good deal better than his ability as an administrator. However, he could more than adequately hold his own in arguments with the leading figures of the day; even, indeed, with the Queen herself. Drake was, in a word, eloquent – and never more so than when addressing his sailors.

Consequently, he was not considered to be a humble sailor who, in times of war, required a more gentlemanly soldier to show him how to fight. During his voyage around the world, to demonstrate he was at once soldier and sailor, he carried the rank of general. During the battle with the Spanish Armada, he held the rank of vice-admiral, but this was only temporary. Like other admirals, he held the position for a particular assignment. Afterwards, he dropped it.

He was a man of style. In the *Golden Hind*, he dined off silver dishes and employed a small orchestra to play at mealtimes. He liked dressing up and, on shore, was considered to be something of a dandy. As a self-made

Map showing the route of Drake's voyage around the world in 1577.

Although Drake (*below*) cared for his seamen and was popular with them, his ships were often inadequately provisioned for the long voyages he undertook.

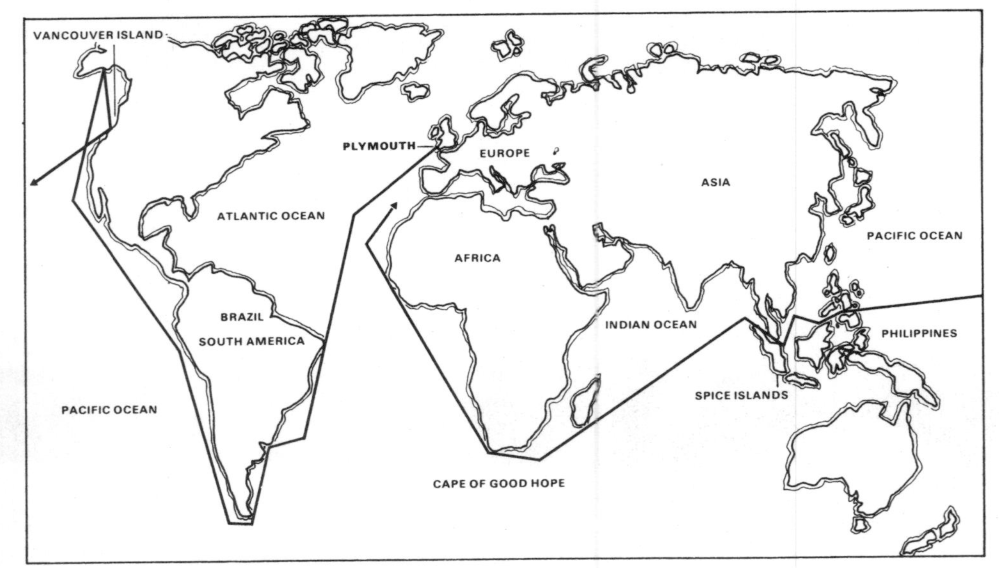

man, he did not, however, consider that class conferred any privileges at sea. Among the members of the *Golden Hind*'s complement was a party of gentlemen-adventurers, who shared his table at meals. But if they expected an easy passage, they were to be disappointed. "I must," he told them, "have the gentlemen to haul and draw with the mariners, and the mariners with the gentlemen. What, let us show ourselves to be all of one company and let us not give occasion to the enemy to rejoice at our decay and overthrow."

Shortly before the expedition entered the Magellan Strait, he ordered the execution of one of the gentlemen, Thomas Doughty – ostensibly because Doughty was suspected of practising witchcraft; but also because he was thought to be stirring up trouble between his companions and the seamen.

The *Golden Hind* carried a crew of eighty men. Among them were a parson, a surgeon, a master-gunner, a boatswain, a carpenter, a cook, and quartermasters who steered the vessel by means of a lever attached to the tiller. The seamen fought as well as sailed: there were no archers. Indeed the old days of soldiers lending their talents to sailors had gone for good. The pattern of a modern warship had been established – though the *Golden Hind*, like most of her contemporaries, was really an armed merchant ship. The establishment of most Tudor ships included a captain, a lieutenant, a master, a pilot (Drake recruited his as he went along – usually Portuguese mariners taken off prize vessels), boatswain, gunner, trumpeter, surgeon, corporal, coxswain, quartermaster, cooper and a cook.

A journey-ring, an early navigational instrument of the type probably used by Drake.

The cleanliness of the ship was in the hands of two seamen: one of whom was known as a "swabber" – the other, a "liar." According to Captain John Smith, "The Swabber is to wash and clean the ship. The liar is to hold his place for but a week, and he that is first taken with a lie every Monday is so proclaimed at the main mast by a general cry of a Liar, a Liar, a Liar; he is under the Swabber and only to clean the beak-head chains."

An artist's impression of a sailor employed by Drake in the sixteenth century.

Presumably, a ship in which all the crew spoke the truth, was not very clean.

The Shape of the World

Once Drake had sailed round the world, it became necessary to re-draw the maps. Magellan, when he penetrated into the Pacific, had not suspected he was near a stretch of ocean extending to the Antarctic. He believed, as others had done, that a large continent lay to the south. Bearing the name of Terra Australis Incognita (the Unknown land of the South Wind), it was said to be rich in gold and silver. At some point, a limb of land was supposed to grope northwards into the Pacific towards New Guinea. Marco Polo was one explorer who had favoured the idea.

Drake's purpose, as originally expressed by him, had been to discover Terra Incognita; and then to sail up the west coast of America in the hope of finding another passage leading back to the Atlantic. It was not conceived as a voyage to circumnavigate the world so much as a circumnavigation of the North and South American continents.

That mercenary monarch, Queen Elizabeth I, who was a shareholder in the undertaking, held no such highfaluting ideas of exploration. She was only interested in the cash return on her investment (like the other backers, she received £47 for every £1 share). It may be significant that, despite Drake's assurances that here, indeed, was a new route to the east, she preferred to salt away her profit in the Levant Company; an organization which continued the old practice of taking the cargoes overland from the eastern end of the Mediterranean.

Due to a storm, which blew his ship off course as she emerged from the Magellan Strait, Drake demolished the myth of Terra Incognita more or less by accident. Instead of a vast and rich continent, he found only a scattering of islands, with Cape Horn at the southernmost point. He called them the Elizabethides. It was left to a Dutch explorer, Wilhelm Cornelius Schouten, to give this stormy outpost the name of his hometown in Holland, Hoorn, in 1516.

Problems of Morale

Long voyages such as these posed problems of discipline and morale among the sailors. Ships may have changed in the following centuries, but the sea has always been the same. To confine a company of eighty or so men in a small ship, little more than 200 tons in size, might seem to be a

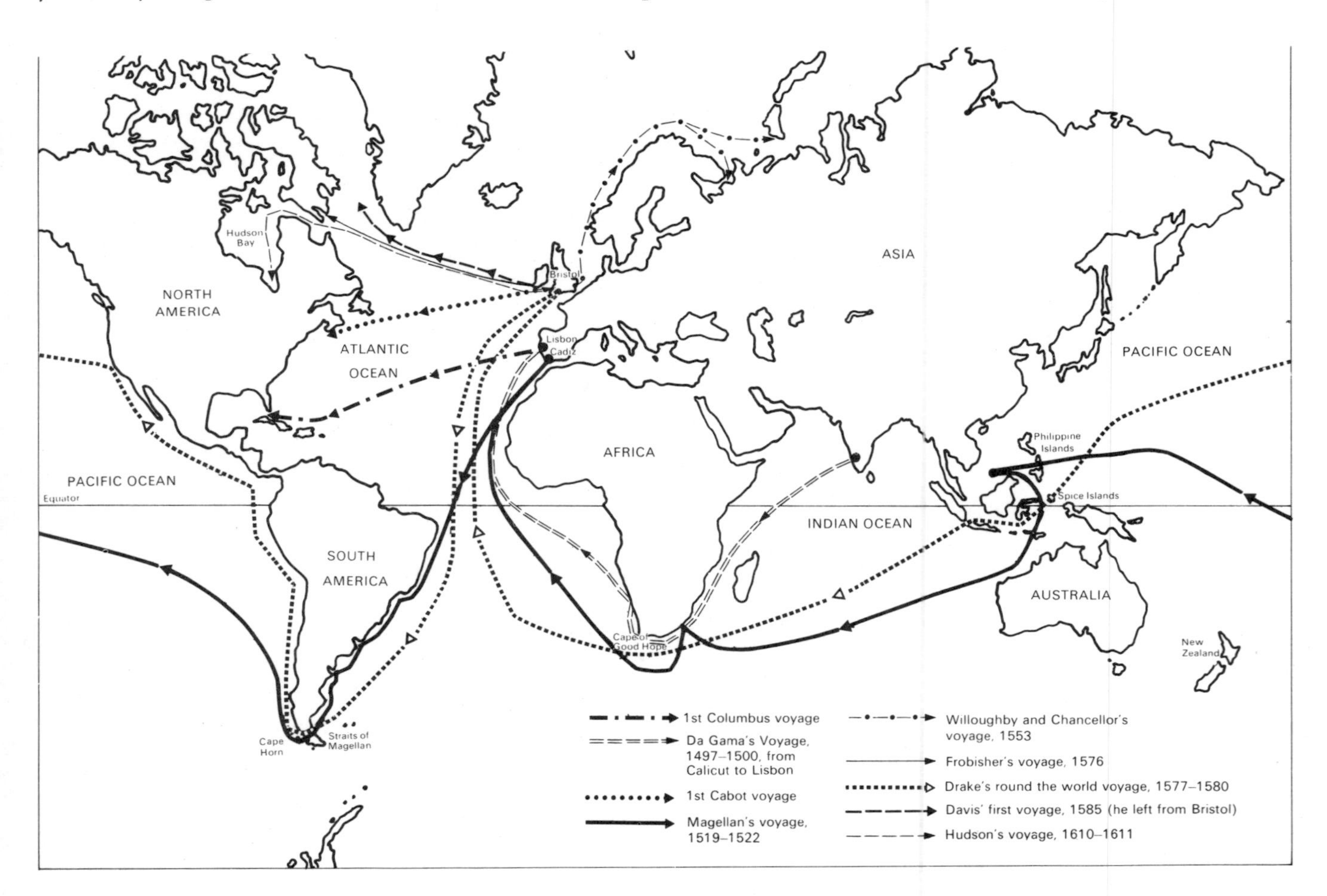

Map showing the routes taken by the early navigators.

Thomas Doughty (his head is seen in the picture) was executed during Drake's voyage around the world because he made trouble between the "gentlemen" adventurers and the "common" sailors.

dangerous undertaking. To cut them off from the normal amenities of life for months – even years – often in foul weather, with poor food and little pay, appears to be a sure way of producing a mutiny. Some of Magellan's men tried it, and were hanged for their pains. Drake's execution of Thomas Doughty may well have been a demonstration of what would lie in store for trouble-makers.

But these assumed the worst. Most commanders had codes of conduct, which they expected the men to observe. Sir John Hawkins's instructions were simple. He told his sailors to:

Serve God daily.
Love one another.
Preserve your victuals.
Beware of fire.
Keep good company.

The object of the voyage for which Sir John composed these exhortations was to further the slave trade.

Before setting out in his search for a north east passage, Sir Hugh Willoughby had ordered that "no blaspheming of God, or detestable swearing, be used in any ship, nor communications of ribaldry, filthy tales, or ungodly talk to be suffered in the company of any ship, neither dicing, carding, tabling, or other devilish game to be frequented, whereby ensureth not only poverty to the players, but also strife, variance, brawling, fighting, and oftentimes murder." Punishments continued harsh. The most common were flogging and ducking from the main yard arm; but captains seem to have exercised devilish ingenuity in dreaming up more elaborate tortures.

One, described by Nathaniel Boteler, was particularly cruel. "The punishment of the capstan," he wrote, "is when a capstan bar being thrust through the hole of the barrel, the offender's arms are extended at the full length cross-wise, and so tied unto the bar, having sometimes a basket of bullets, or some other like weight hanging by his neck; in which posture he continueth till he be either brought to confess some plot or crime, whereof he is frequently suspected; or that he hath received such suffering as he is censured to undergo at the discretion of the captain."

Petty theft and similar crimes were punished by the whip, with the malefactor tied to the capstan; "and the knaveries of the ship boys [Boteler wrote] were payd by the Boat-swain with the rod; and commonly this execution is done on the Munday mornings; and is so frequently in use that some meer seamen believe in ernest that they shall not have a fair wind, unless the boys be duely brought to the chest, that is to be whipped every Munday morning."

After this almost ritual flogging was over, according to Captain John Smith in his *Seaman's Grammar*, the boys were "to have a quarter can of beer and a brisket of bread." The less fortunate, presumably, had to take this nourishment standing up.

Many of the sailors were excellent men, but there were exceptions. When, during the reign of Henry VII, a vessel named the *Mary Rose* capsized at Spithead, her commander called his crew "a sort of knaves." Apparently, they "so maligned and disdayned one another that, refusing to doe that which they should doe, and so contendinge in spite, perished in frowardnesse." One Elizabethan captain described his men as a "loose rabble;" another called them "vagrant, lewd and disorderly;" and, from a third, "a ragged regiment of common rogues."

In an attempt to attract a better type of man into the profession, Sir Richard Hawkins, Treasurer to the Admiralty, urged an improvement in the scale of pay. A master was to receive £26.8½ a month; a boatswain, £10.86; and so on – the most poorly paid was the mariner, who was only given £6.50. By this, he hoped that "Her majesty's ships would be furnished with able men, such as can shift for themselves, keep themselves clean from vermin or noisomness, which breedeth sickness and mortality."

On the face of it, the new pay structure appeared to be generous. Richard Burbage, the star of the London theatre at about this time, was said to be worth £300 a year (£25 a month), which has been described as "a small fortune for those days." Less than a century later, a good

The defeat of the Spanish Armada in 1588.

husbandman (farmer) in Lancashire was said to be receiving only £3 a year, and a leading landowner paid his bailiff a mere four pounds. The fact that these men received living accommodation and food is hardly relevant. The sailors were also assured of their keep. Nor was the suggestion that seafarers led much harder lives a valid reason for the huge difference. The husbandman had to be up at three o'clock in the morning to tend his animals. However, the navy's pay was an artful mixture of fact and fiction. It was one thing to lay down a wages scale, and quite another to ensure that the men received the money. Among the paymasters and pursers, there were plenty of conniving characters only too ready to defraud the sailors. It may not have been a coincidence that, when he died in 1622, the cause of Sir Richard's death was said to be "vexation."

Appalling Conditions

A seaman was poorly paid: and badly fed. The rations stipulated in the Elizabethan period were a pound of biscuits, a gallon of beer, and a pound of meat per man on four days a week. For the other three, the men were issued with cheese and dried fish. On active service, however, these amounts were halved in an attempt to maintain stocks. Furthermore, the quality of the food was frequently below standard. It was small wonder that there was a good deal of illness on shipboard, and an ever present danger of mutiny.

Even after the successful foray to Cadiz, the captain and crew of one of

Overleaf. Crew of the *Ark Royal* during the Armada. Artist's impression.

W.H.Overend 88

Drake's ships (the *Golden Lyon*) refused to obey his orders. In a message to the commander-in-chief, the vessel's master, John Marchaunt, wrote: "Wee, the Quenes and yours at this tyme desyre, that, as you are a man and beare the name of a captayne over us, so to weighe of us like men, and lett us not be spoyled for wante of food, for our allowaunce is so smale we are not able to lyve any longer of it." They were, he wrote, weak from lack of nourishment – a condition which "suerly if it be not loked into, will growe to great dishonour on your parte, and to lasting shayme on our sydes."

As the *Golden Lyon* made her own way back to Britain, while the rest of the squadron sailed south to the Azores, Drake tried the mutineers in their absence. He sentenced them to death. When the matter was looked into by a court of inquiry set up by the Queen, however, the verdict was quashed.

Cures for a Seaman's Ills

The food in Drake's ships was notoriously bad. It would, however, be unjust to take him to task too severely: he was merely following the example of his sovereign. In 1588 when, surely, the Queen's sailors ought to have been enjoying rewards for their success against the Armada, many of them were lying seriously ill. And some of them were dying. The reason was that Elizabeth I, that most parsimonious of monarchs, was too mean to ensure that her vessels carried adequate supplies of food. The fare on board them was less than the bare necessities of life required. Consequently, many of the mariners were suffering from malnutrition.

Provisioning a ship for the long voyages was always a problem. Months often went by without fresh food and what was stored on board quickly went bad.

Whatever hardships Drake's seamen endured from inadequate rations, their commander at least took the trouble to concern himself with other matters concerning their health. On the *Golden Hind*'s voyage, he inspected them regularly; and, when the vessel was in Equatorial waters, he bled them in the belief that it would keep them in better condition. Down in the Magellan Straits, one of his captains – John Wynter – was walking along the shore one day, when he noticed that some of the evergreen trees had an aromatic bark. Thinking that it might be good for scurvy, he took a supply back on board with him. Its success as a remedy is not recorded; but it has gone down to posterity in botanical circles as *Drimys Winteri* (Winter's bark).

When Anson sailed round the world in the early 1740s, Philip Saumarez, who commanded the *Centurion* and had a scientific turn of mind, came across a rich haul of medicine on the island of Juan Fernandez (the reputed desert island of Robinson Crusoe) in the South Pacific. A large myrtle tree, he discovered, "bore an excrescence like moss, growing on a small stock on the bark of the tree whose taste and smell resembled garlic, and was used by us as such. The tree excreted likewise the polipody which we found a good laxitive. . . . We found a small shrub somewhat like the tilibri cherry bark tree whose bark we used as an astringent with great success as well as the pelliberry which we discovered in great quantities and is looked on as a nitrous duiretic."

It was, virtually, a botanical chemists shop: though one cannot help wondering who was the first to try the discoveries. Nobody, certainly, seems to have been poisoned by them.

Elizabeth I (*left*) was happy to enjoy the glory won by English sailor adventurers – and a large share of the profits of the voyages – but did little for her sailors and was too mean to maintain a permanent navy.

But the most important gap in the mariner's medicine chest was a cure for scurvy – or, better still, something which would prevent it. None would have been more grateful for this than the captain of the *Centurion*; for, when his ship was crossing the Pacific, the death rate was seldom less than twelve men a day. Another vessel, the *Gloucester*, lost 327 members of her 400-strong crew from the disease. The first symptoms were spots on the gums. These were followed by bleeding and, before long, the victim's teeth began to fall out. Sores appeared on the skin: a tremendous lethargy overwhelmed the patient, and any sudden movement of the body usually had fatal consequences. According to one estimate, no fewer than 10,000 sailors died of the disease during Queen Elizabeth's reign.

At first, people put the complaint down to changes in the climate. Sir Richard Hawkins then made the discovery that oranges and lemons had a remedial effect. This was confirmed in 1600, when Sir James Lancaster led a squadron of ships to India. Sir James had taken some bottles of lemon juice; and, during the voyage, his crew was the only one to escape the illness. A spoonful, taken every morning, was the right dose: "the juice worketh much better if the party keep a short diet and wholly

These Portuguese carracks were built early in the sixteenth century. Portugal and Spain dominated the seas before the coming of Hawkins and Drake.

refrain salt meat, which salt meat, and long being at sea, is the only cause of the breeding of this disease."

Both Hawkins and Lancaster had discovered a cure, without fully understanding the cause. Scurvy comes from a deficiency of vitamin C in the diet. By dosing their men with the juice of lemons, these commanders were making up for the lack of fresh vegetables on board ship.

The East India Company

When Drake captured the Portuguese treasure ship, *San Felipe*, off the Azores in 1588, he helped himself and his sovereign to £114,000's worth of loot. The Spaniards and Portuguese, not unnaturally, branded him as a pirate. The English Queen preferred to think of him as a national hero. She could scarcely have held any other opinion; for Her Majesty, more than anyone else, was being well rewarded by Sir Francis's somewhat irregular actions on the high seas. Had she been compelled to justify his conduct, she would no doubt have pointed to the very fine line which separated a pirate from a privateer.

Whilst the former was a criminal, the latter followed an entirely respectable occupation. In times of war, privateers formed the backbone of the navy; in peacetime, syndicates, often headed by the sovereign, financed the fitting out of their ships. As for the sailors, they were only too eager to serve in these vessels. The normal pay was, in all conscience, small enough. Working in a privateer, on the other hand, entitled a mariner to a share of the swag. As one observer wrote, "As for the business of pillage, there is nothing that more bewitcheth them, nor anything wherein they promise themselves so loudly, nor delight in more mainly."

The more obvious reward for taking the *San Felipe* was a cargo of precious stones. The less apparent – but, in the long run, infinitely more important – was a document in the captain's cabin. The ship was on her way home from a voyage to the East Indies, and this collection of papers supplied a record of her trading activities. It confirmed what a number of people had suspected: there was a great deal of money to be made from the east.

Eleven years later, the *San Felipe*'s records caused a new joint stock company to be formed with the Queen's approval. It was called the East India Company.

The merchants of those days fell into two classes. One comprised the so-called "regulated companies," in which each member traded with his own capital. The Merchant Adventurers, who specialised in the export of cloth, came into this category. The other type was the joint stock company. The East India Company, the African Company and, later, the Hudson's Bay Company, are typical examples. Each was assigned a sphere of operations by Royal Charter: and, within that sphere, each had a complete monopoly. A great deal of money was required to finance them: for, in the farther-flung corners of the world, they could expect no help from the navy or the army. Consequently, in addition to their trading activities, they had to support their own fighting services.

In peacetime ships belonged to merchants (*above*) and were used for trading purposes. In wartime both ship and crew had to be handed over to the sovereign.

When the ageing Queen Elizabeth gave the East India Company its charter, she presented it to the Earl of Cumberland and two hundred knights. It was for a period of fifteen years. Among the privileges it conferred were the exemption of import and export duties on its goods; concessions to export bullion; and permission for six ships and six pinnaces with a complement of 500 men to sail annually. The company's original capital totalled £72,000. Five ships were acquired in 1600 (among them James Lancaster's), and 480 sailors were recruited.

In 1609, when it became clear that the charter was going to be renewed for another fifteen years, the company embarked on a shipbuilding programme. The biggest vessel on order was the *Trade's Increase*. Registering 1,200 tons, she was the largest merchantman that had ever been built in Britain. Opinions about the *Golden Hind*'s tonnage vary: one estimate suggests that she was only 120-tons, though this is probably on the conservative side. Although she had been built less than one hundred years (the actual date is unknown) before the *Trade's Increase*, she was a mere midget beside the newcomer. More important to the sailors was that all the East Indiamen carried large supplies of lemon juice on board, no doubt at Sir James Lancaster's insistence. Consequently, scurvy became nothing more than an unpleasant memory. The Admiralty were less progressive. Their Lordships regarded the complaint as just another hazard of the deep: something which was inevitable and, therefore, had to be tolerated.

Possibly they considered Lancaster a crank; and preferred the view of one writer, who suggested that: "It may be conceived, I say, that the steams arising from the ocean may have a tendency to render the air they are spread through less properly adapted to the support of life of terrestrial animals, unless those streams are corrected by effluvia of another kind, and which perhaps the land alone can supply." Or, perhaps, they were reluctant to invest in the cost of lemons.

3 *A Sailor's Lot*

. . . was, like that of W. S. Gilbert's policeman, not a happy one. When the East India Company insisted that all its ships should carry supplies of lemon juice on board, the incidence of scurvy dropped dramatically. But was even this enlightened organization paying sufficient attention to the diet of its hardworking mariners? According to Captain John Smith, who published his *Seaman's Grammar* in 1627, no shipowner – and this included the Admiralty – was concerning itself sufficiently with the health and well-being of its crews.

Wrote the gallant Captain (who, incidentally, founded the state of Virginia in America): "Some it may be well say I would have men feast than fight, but I say the want of these necessaries occasions the loss of more men than in any English fleet hath been slain since eighty-eight [the year of the Armada]. For when a man is ill, or at the point of death, I would know whether a dish of buttered rice with a little cinnamon, ginger and sugar, a little minced meat or roast beef, a few stewed prunes brewed with a little cinnamon and sugar, be not better than a little Poor John or salt fish with oil and mustard, or biscuit, butter and cheese or oatmeal pottage on fishdays, or on fleshdays salt beef, pork and pease with six shilling beer, that is your ordinary ship's allowance, and good for them that are well conditioned, which is not always, as seamen can too well witness."

Among the provisions, Captain Smith insisted, should be spices, Dutch cheese, wine, bacon, mutton, jam, and lemon juice. It was a pious, if impracticable, hope. The pursers who, working with catering contractors, were responsible for provisions, had few scruples about supplementing their incomes at the sailors' cost. One long standing racket was to weigh out fourteen ounces and call the product a pound. The remaining two ounces was reckoned to be profit. As for the cooks: on the pay scale, they were one grade higher than seamen, but this was not a tribute to their culinary talents. Long John Silver of *Treasure Island* personifies a good many sea-cooks of the period. They were men chosen because they had some disability or other, which prevented them from performing the normal duties of mariners. Most of them had neither the skill nor the enthusiasm to fashion such dainty dishes as Captain Smith had in mind.

The scale of pay for sailors was laid down in official documents. On the other hand, the authorities were less concerned to see that the men

Opposite. Ships of the East India Company. The Company was the first English trading company to have a regular service to the East. When it started, at the beginning of the seventeenth century, the incidence of scurvy among its crews was reduced because the Company supplied them with fresh lemon juice during voyages.

actually received it. In 1666, for example, there were a number of mariners who had not received any money for two years. Some men-of-war, when advertising for recruits, offered cash-on-the-nail as an incentive. Others guaranteed, or professed to, that arrears of pay would be promptly made up.

Insisting on Their Rights

Some seamen, not unjustly, insisted on their rights. In 1652, a Captain Thomas Thorowgood made this report to a Navy Commissioner: "These are to give Your Worship notice that on Saturday last, I tendered our sailors down six months pay, which they refused to take, saying that they have all or none, and rated upon Your Worship and myself and the rest of the owners, saying you had received all the ship's pay of the state and that Your Worship and myself were about to cheat them of their wages, and swore they would have it or else the ship should lie there and rot; and they are grown to such a height that they will not be at my command, but do what they please, for on Saturday night they were singing and roaring, and I sent my servant to bid the boatswain to be quiet and go to their cabins, but they would not, so I went down myself and desired them to give over and go to their cabins, but they told me they would not be at my command, so I struck one of them, and the rest put out the candle and took hold of me as though they would have torn me to pieces, so that I am almost beside myself, not knowing what to do. I could with all my heart wish the ship [which was at Portsmouth] were at London, and you knew how to deal with them."

The battle between the Dutch and English fleets at Solebay in 1672. The Dutch had a greater shipbuilding capacity than Britain, and their ships could be handled by smaller crews.

The *Resolution*, a ship of the line, caught in a storm in 1667. Climbing the rigging to take in sail in rough weather was hard and dangerous work.

Captain Thorowgood, we must assume, ran neither a tight ship nor a happy one. Unfortunately, he was by no means an exception. During the Dutch wars of the seventeenth century, there were many seamen who made unfavourable comparisons between conditions in their own vessels, and in those of the enemy.

Sir Francis Drake had made it abundantly clear that mariners could be trained to fight as well as sail. He had, in a manner of speaking, become the prototype naval officer. Nevertheless, vestiges of the old system remained. During the second war against the Dutch (1665–7), which was brought about by conflicts over trade with Africa and America, naval warfare became fashionable. A young blade about town liked to boast that he had seen combat on the high seas. Reflecting the attitude of the gentlemen adventurers who sailed in the *Golden Hind*, he offered his services to the Admiralty. Invariably, he was rewarded with the rank of lieutenant – or, if he had sufficient influence, he might even be given the command of a ship.

Comforts of Officer Life

When he went to sea, he tried to take with him all the comforts of life on shore. Rather than accept the rough-and-ready fare concocted by the ship's cook, a number employed French chefs. Valets, musicians, tailors, artists, footmen and dogs were among other unlikely appointments to a ship's company. Food was the most important consideration. The gentlemen ate well on shore, and they were determined to live equally well at sea. Henry Teonge, a naval chaplain who saw service on board a man-of-war in 1675, found that the rigours of a storm in the Mediterranean were made tolerable by the menu. According to E. S. Turner, "the officers consume their quota of Zante beef and fat pullets and drink all the appropriate toasts, their legs braced against the furniture."

On Christmas Day, Teonge noted in his diary, he and his colleagues "ate not so great a dinner as was intended." This was due to the fact that the supply of fresh beef had run out. However, they did not go hungry. The fare included rice pudding, neat's tongue, cabbage, fried fish, woodcock pie, two roast hens, cheese, blue figs, and a great deal of wine and punch. In an East Indiaman of the period, there was so much livestock on deck and in the lifeboats, that the vessel is said to have resembled a "floating farmyard." In harbour, of course, the living became more riotous. At a Turkish port, Teonge and his colleagues were entertained by the British Consul. "At every health that we drank," the parson wrote, "every man broke the glass that he drank in; so that before night we had destroyed a whole chest of pure Venice glasses."

The fact that these officers knew absolutely nothing about seamanship was not held to be a disadvantage. George Monk, Duke of Albemarle, was more accustomed to handling horses than he was to commanding a man-of-war. Consequently, he was apt to give the command "Charge!" when his vessel went into battle. He was also in the habit of instructing the helmsman "to turn the wheel to the right" – a habit which infuriated the professional seamen. The Duke had, admittedly, joined the Navy to escape the consequences of having thrashed the under-sheriff of Devon; but his nautical amateurism was not exceptional.

Thus class distinction occurred again. Just as the early warships had employed soldiers and sailors – with the former regarded as the social superiors of the latter, so did ships' officers now fall into two categories. There were Gentlemen (or "Fairweather") Officers and the more lowly "Tarpaulins." As Macaulay very rightly said, "There were gentlemen and there were seamen in the Navy of Charles II. But the seamen were not gentlemen and the gentlemen were not seamen."

The King was inclined to favour the gentlemen; for, he believed, the more coarse-grained tarpaulins lacked the social graces required of a transient ambassador when a British ship put in at a foreign port. The fact that the vessel had to get there in the first place seemed to be a matter of small importance.

Nor were the higher members of society notably courageous. One case was reported of a gentleman who was so terrified when his ship went into action, that he always dived for cover below deck. Aware that this aroused the scorn of his companions, and not without shame, he ordered himself to be tied to the mast on these occasions. Captain George Carleton, who wrote about the incident, observed: "To be tied from running away can import nothing less than that he would have continued these signs of cowardice if he had not been prevented. There is a bravery of mind which, I fancy, few of these gentlemen . . . are possessed of."

Admiral Herbert, the Earl of Torrington, commanded his fleet from a flagship which, on account of its splendours and debaucheries, was known as "a little Versailles." His captains were required to dress him

A woodcut made in 1613 showing the bosun's chair, an early way of rescuing someone who had fallen overboard.

and comb his wig, which was degrading enough. The unkindest cut of all, however, was administered by the House of Lords. When his lordship was court martialled for losing the Battle of Beachy Head in 1690 (which resulted in the French fleet being able to command the English Channel without opposition) the House opposed it. Tarpaulins, its members said, were not worthy of sitting in judgement on a peer of the realm.

Perhaps the unhappiest fate of a gentleman officer was that of a country squire named Hodge Vaughan. Mr. Vaughan was wounded during the early stages of an engagement. Somebody carried him below; and, for a few hours, he was forgotten. When next seen, only a few remains of this luckless officer were to be found. He had, it seemed, been eaten alive by the ship's supply of wild pigs, which had been starved out of their minds.* His equals may have mourned him: the professional sailors were possibly less distressed. The two classes seldom had any great regard for each other.

Control of the Navy

King John, back in the thirteenth century, had been the first monarch to create any system of control over the running of the navy. Improbably, perhaps, he appointed a parson to the job – William de Wrotham, Archdeacon of Taunton, who was compelled to neglect his ecclesiastical duties for the work of Clerk of the Ships. Henry VIII appointed a board of

* The Lord High Admiral (James, Duke of York) insisted that, as an alternative to beef, the sailors should be issued with "one pound over dupois bacon, or salted English pork of a well-fed hog, and a pint of pease" on two days a week.

commissioners to handle the routine affairs of the Navy, and these men, seven all told, were responsible to the Lord High Admiral. The power of this official depended on who was the Head of State. Charles I for instance, gave the first Duke of Buckingham a great deal of authority. During the Commonwealth, and appropriate to rule by Parliament the responsibilities were vested in a panel of eleven men, who carried the title of Commissioners for Managing the Affairs of the Admiralty and Navy. When Charles II was restored to monarchy in 1660, he re-introduced the position; but, then, Charles had a considerable personal interest in the Navy (he was, incidentally, the first sovereign to own a royal yacht). He gave the job of Lord High Admiral to his brother and heir, James – Duke of York. James cannot have had an easy time of it. The King was inclined to meddle. Beneath him, in the capacity of Clerk of the Ships, was Samuel Pepys: a civil servant described by Oliver Warner in *The Navy* as "one of the shrewdest men who ever devoted his talents to the Fleet." He, far more than the Lord High Admiral or even the monarch, created the shape of the modern Navy.

Although best-known for his *Diary*, Samuel Pepys (*below right*) did much to lay the foundations for Britain's future naval power. As Secretary to the Admiralty he reorganized the navy in a more efficient and businesslike way. Pepys was particularly concerned to improve conditions for the ordinary seamen (*below*).

Pepys had a considerable admiration for sailors. "Towards showing the hardships of the seaman's trade," he wrote, "it is mighty observable the strange difficulties they suffer in the dark nights in storms, when men must go up to hand their sails etcetera in the night."

After the Four Days Battle of 1666, in which the Dutch inflicted a crushing defeat on the English, Pepys was beseiged at the Admiralty by

women whose husbands were prisoners in Holland. "I confess," he wrote, "their cries were so sad for money, and laying down the condition of their families and their husbands, and what they have done and suffered for the King, and how ill they are used by us. . . . I do most heartily pity them, and was ready to cry to hear them."

The Making of a Professional Officer

The officer situation was obviously a source of much discomfort to a man with such a logical mind as Pepys. The system of employing two types, gentlemen and tarpaulins, was absurd. Neither the fop nor the ancient mariner was precisely what the service needed. The ideal fell somewhere between the two: a man who was not only a good seaman, but who was also reasonably well-educated. The qualities he demanded were "downright diligence, sobriety, and seamanship," and the product of them would be a professional naval officer.

In 1686, Pepys assumed the title of Navy Secretary, and announced his reforms. The newcomers to the service were to be known as King's Letter boys. Although they were actually cadets, they were classed as midshipmen. These were not men-about-town who joined the Navy casually and, equally casually, left it once the glamour of a life at sea had worn thin. They were career officers. They signed on at the age of eleven or upwards; came from good families; and were subjected to rigorous training. Anyone who aspired to become lieutenant had to put in a

The Custom House beside the River Thames in the City of London. Designed by Christopher Wren, it was the first building visited by a ship's master when his vessel arrived in the port.

The press gang was feared in all towns near the coasts. To supplement voluntary recruitment, gangs were employed to "impress" – in fact, to abduct men to serve in the navy.

required amount of service, and then take an exam at the Navy Office.

There were, of course, a number of people who protested that such requirements offended the divine right of the upper classes; that their privileges should safeguard them from the rougher aspects of discipline at sea and the need to pass exams. But these voices were in the minority.

The Press Gang

Some of the men on the lower deck entered the service because they wished to: many were pressed in to it. What with bad food, irregular pay, harsh discipline and a good deal of danger, the life had few attractions. Those who set their hearts on going to sea preferred to entrust their well-being to merchantmen. In peacetime, Pepys, who was a humane man, was against impressment. In wartime, even he had to acknowledge that it was essential. During the Dutch wars, for instance, the strength of the Navy had to be increased from 3,000 men to 30,000. There was only one way in which to fill the gap, and that was to compel men to join.

Among the more articulate critics of impressment was Daniel Defoe. In his *Review of the Affairs of France with Observations and Transactions at Home*, he demanded that the system should be abolished. "Why," he asked, "should a brute, a mere tar, a drunken sailor, judge by the force of his cudgel, who is, or who is not, fit for public service at sea?" In fact, pressed men were able to appeal against their fate by a due process of law. Few of them took advantage of it – possibly because they did not understand their rights; and, almost certainly, because most of them realized how badly their services were needed.

The press gang was one of the oldest and most sinister features of naval history. The gang leader (often a retired naval captain) was issued with a warrant, which entitled him to round up men for the fleet. He and his men were paid on a kind of commission basis. Once they had seized hold of their victim, the object was to force him to accept a shilling. The acceptance of the sovereign's money in this way formed a contract, and the men were thereafter bound to serve.

In fact, by no means everyone received his shilling. The gang leader or his men were not above appropriating the cash; and Pepys recalls paying seamen out of his own pocket – simply because the "presters" claimed that they had run out of cash.

Ships at sea were by no means exempt from the press gangs, though the gangs were discouraged from interfering with vessels which were outward bound. With so much piracy about, they were deemed to need their full complement. Homeward bound crews were another matter. In 1670, for instance, no fewer than fifty men were taken off colliers in the Downs off the coast of Kent.

There were only a few exemptions. Thames watermen, apprentices, crews of mayoral barges and employees of Trinity House were among them: and every merchant ship was allowed to retain a fixed proportion of her crew. The gangs were not allowed to function in the City of London without the assent of the Lord Mayor. Otherwise, any sailor was fair game – and, indeed, non-sailors, too. Magistrates were inclined to ease the pressure on the nation's gaols by delivering felons and vagrants into the arms of the presters.

The first few days of an impressed man's life were dreadful. He was taken aboard a tender and thrown into the hold. The hatch was battened down to prevent his escape, and marines mounted guard outside. There were no sanitary arrangements; the movement of the vessel on rough waters was unpleasant; the stench abominable; the company, with its criminal element, undesirable; and, as a breeding ground for disease, it had few equals. In theory, once he had boarded the tender, a man was entitled to buy an outfit of clothing – and he was also entitled to pay for it out of his wages. The state made no contribution. But, since sailors seldom received their pay, it was equally seldom that money and clothes changed hands. What was more to the point, perhaps, was that there were no adequate catering arrangements. A man spent anything up to forty-eight hours in this hell ship, and went hungry for most of it. However, this may have been bearable, for the conditions were hardly conducive to a good appetite.

A list of fifteen instructions was prepared by the Admiralty for the lieutenants who commanded the tenders. Among them was this: "You are to take care that every man on board be as well accommodated with lodgings as the vessel will allow, and that they all have His Majesty's full allowance of provisions daily; and if the copper be so small that one boiling will not suffice, to order a second or more boilings if necessary." The intention behind the orders may have been a good one. Unfortunately, the orders were rarely carried out.

Attracting Volunteers

Pressed men were unpopular with ships' captains – all of whom preferred volunteers. In an effort to obtain the right type of man, posters were displayed in ports. The wording was a triumph of the copy writer's art. Had there been such a thing at the time, it would also have been a flagrant breach of the Trade Descriptions Act. For example, during the war against France, which followed the French Revolution, men (with or without seafaring experience) were invited to enlist at Shoreham in Sussex. Beneath the Royal coat of arms appeared the following: "Let us, who are Englishmen, protect and defend our good KING and COUNTRY against the Attempts of all *Republicans* and *Levellers*, and against the Designs of our NATURAL ENEMIES, who intend this Year to invade OLD ENGLAND our *happy Country*, to murder our gracious KING [George III] as they have done their own; to make WHORES of our *Wives* and *Daughters*; to rob us of our PROPERTY; and to teach us nothing but the *damn'd Art* of murdering one another.

"ROYAL TARS of OLD ENGLAND, If you love your COUNTRY, and your LIBERTY, Now is the time to show your Love. REPAIR [to Lieutenant W. J. Stephens at Shoreham] where you will be allowed to enter for any SHIP of WAR."

Before getting down to more practical details, the writer allowed himself a further burst of rhetoric: "All who have good Hearts," he wrote, "who love their KING, their COUNTRY, and RELIGION, who hate the FRENCH, and damn the POPE" were invited to take advantage of the invitation. Their fares to Shoreham would be paid: their chests and bedding would be sent "carriage free," and they would receive the following bounties:

An Able-bodied seaman – £5.00
An Ordinary Seaman – £2.50
And a land-lubber – £1.50

For promises, promises, promises, however, there was little to beat another poster issued in the reign of George III. It offered volunteers handsome bounties and: "Advantages superior to any other Service, viz The Families and Friends of Volunteers will receive Monthly Pay, and the Volunteers themselves will have a bountiful Supply of CLOTHING, BEEF, GROG, FLIP [a mixture of hot small beer laced with brandy and sweetened with spice], and STRONG BEER, also a Certainty of PRIZE MONEY as the men entered for this service will be sent to capture The Rich Spanish Galleons and in Consequence will return loaded with DOLLARS and HONOURS to spend their days in PEACE and PLENTY. HUZZA!!"

The writer appears to have confused his periods: the reference to

Opposite. A water spout – one of the sea's most terrifying phenomena.

"Rich Spanish Galleons" would have been appropriate in Drake's day: in the late eighteenth century, the rewards may have been more meagre. Nevertheless, there was no doubting its appeal to the impoverished citizens in the three Lancashire towns where it was displayed.

Duties on Board Ship

For details of the men's duties during a voyage we are indebted to that maritime sage, Captain John Smith. The crew were divided into two categories according to age. "The Sailors," he wrote, "are the ancient men for hoisting the sails, getting the tacks on board, hauling the bowline and steering the ship.

"The Younkers are the young men called Fore Mast Men to take in the top falls, or top and yard, for furling the sails, and slinging the yards (pulling and tricing up), and take their turns at the helm."

The ship's company was organized into two watches: the Larboard (now "port" – otherwise known as the boatswain's) and starboard (or master's). Within them, the seamen were formed into smaller groups under the mates. "You are to mess them four to a Mess," Captain Smith continued, "and then give every Mess a quarter can of beer and bisket of bread to stay their stomachs till the kettle be boiled, and that they may go first to prayer, then to supper, and at six o'clock sing a psalm, say a prayer, and the Master with his side begins the Watch, then all the rest may do what they will till midnight, and then his Mate with his Larboard men, with a psalm and a prayer, relieve them till four in the morning . . . except some sudden flaw of wind come, some storm or gust, or some accident that requires the help of all hands, which commonly after such good cheer in most voyages doth happen."

Storms at Sea

A seaman called Alex Anderson described the kind of thing which *could* happen, in an account which, like the majority of British seamen's accounts, is a masterpiece of understatement. In 1869, Anderson was serving on board a small ship (a mere 130 tons) on passage to Melbourne. She was carrying a cargo of sugar. Her passengers were mostly prospectors bound for Australian gold fields. At some point in the Indian Ocean she ran into a cyclone: "We were now going bows under," Mr. [later Captain] Anderson wrote, "and shipping big and dangerous seas. I, acting as ship's carpenter, had to knock away some of the lower planks from the bulwarks to let the mass of water run off the deck, but the sea, still increasing, carried away the remainder and everything else excepting the bulwark stauncheons. It was impossible to remain on deck without bulwarks, unless lashed to something. The old gold diggers and the sailors sat the night out, side by side, in the little cabin aft, singing hymns at times. . . .

"Daylight came after a weary night. The birds, which had all been scattered by the force of the wind, began again to fly around us. The seas were not by now so white nor breaking so fiercely."

For sheer matter-of-factness, however, it is hard to better a report by Admiral Sir Cloudesley Shovel. He was commanding a squadron of eight ships on the night of 27th November, 1703, when the Great Storm unleashed its fury around the coast of England. The Admiral's vessels were lying in the Downs off the Kent coast. "On Saturday last," he wrote, "soone in the morning wee had a most miserable storm of wind, which drove us to some Streights, for after we had veerrd out more than three cables of our best bower that Anchor broke, soon after our Tillar broke, and before we could secure our Rudder it broke from our sterne, and has shaken our Sterne Port that we prove very leakey, and had our four Chaine Pumps and a hand Pump going to get us free. We let go our Sheete Anchor, and veerrd out all the cables to it, butt that did not ride us, butt wee drove near a sand called the Galloper, of which we saw the breach; I directed the main mast to be cutt by the board, after which we ridd fast. Of eight ships that came out of the Downes, four are missing."

The total score for that disastrous occasion was thirteen men-of-war lost – plus the Eddystone lighthouse, which was destroyed.

But the weather was not the only peril of the deep. In 1652, when the Dutch fleet was abroad in the Channel, a British packet boat took three days to make the short passage between Calais and Rye. Throughout the period, she had been involved in a cat-and-mouse game of dodging unfriendly warships.

4 *Naval Occasions*

The British sailor had much to endure, and he bore it well. Now and then, however, he felt compelled to protest. In 1702, a booklet entitled *An Essay on the Navy* was published. In it, an anonymous author listed a number of complaints. Most of them dealt with cruelty. As it made clear, a sailor's misery did not come only from formal punishments. The lieutenants and the boatswains used to carry sticks about with them. When they saw a seaman idling, or when they felt in a bad temper, they would strike the unfortunate fellow. On a grander scale, the cat-of-three-tails had grown into one of five tails, which, at the end of the seventeenth century, had been replaced by a villainous brute of nine tails.

Perhaps the officers tended to forget that their ships were manned by human beings. The author of *An Essay on the Navy* complained of "the new invented names wherewith some of their commanders and officers constantly call them, viz. *Sons of eternal whores, Bloods of eternal bitches*, etc. And as they call them, so they curse them with such horrid and blasphemous imprecations and language that I even blush to mention." To support his allegations, he printed evidence from "a commander of a merchant ship who had served in the Navy eight years." This gentleman referred to the officers' "manner of cursing the men, viz. *Damn their bloods, they would roast their souls in hell.* Others tell the men they would *Make them curse God and die.*" And so on.

But cruelty was not the only just cause of complaint. By the end of the eighteenth century, the men in the Navy had received no increases in pay since the days of Charles I. During this period of well over one hundred years, the cost of living had roughly doubled.

Mutiny!

In 1797, matters came to a head when the crews at Spithead mutinied. They were due to put to sea on Easter Sunday, when an apparently impromptu cheer was heard coming from the flagship. Within seconds, men on other vessels had joined in. It was a signal for the nautical equivalent of downing tools. They would not, they said, set sail again until their demand for one shilling (5p.) a day increase in pay had been met. They also required an assurance that, when the ships were in port, flour would not be substituted for bread. And: an adequate supply of fresh vegetables; better attention for the sick; a limited amount of shore leave; full pay for men who had been wounded in action; and an

Opposite. Lord Nelson shortly after being hit by a French musket ball. He was taken below with a handkerchief over his face so that the crew would not realize what had happened and so become demoralized.

Sometimes captains went too far with their discipline. Bligh was one: his conduct provoked his crew to mutiny and to set him adrift in the Pacific in a ship's boat.

improvement in pensions to equal those already provided by the Army. There was to be no victimization of the mutineers.

Perhaps the most surprising thing about the Spithead mutiny was its friendliness. When a German prince came to visit the fleet, the men cheerfully rowed him round the various vessels, and he was given the appropriate salutes. When – after inactivity, and then, quibbling – the Admiralty at last produced an acceptable offer, the men's leader, Valentine Joyce, and Earl Howe (the recently retired Commander-in-Chief) discussed it amiably on shore over a few glasses of wine. The outcome was that several of their demands (including pay) were met, and a free pardon was given to the offenders.

A number of officers sympathized with their men. A lieutenant in the *Monarch* wrote, "the seamen still continue to conduct themselves incredibly well. . . . I had always great respect for an English seaman; I like the character now better than ever." And, from another, "They have all, however, excepting one ship only (the flagship of Sir John Colpoys), behaved with great prudence, decency and moderation (if I may use those terms when speaking of an act of mutiny) in this business; and obey their officers as before in the regular routine of ship's duty – saying that they are not dissatisfied with their officers or the service, but are determined to have an increase in pay. . . ."

"As an officer," the writer concluded, "I must condemn their conduct; as a well-wisher to my country, I must regret its being so exceedingly ill-timed; but, as a man, I can find many excuses for them."

The matter might have ended there, if it had not been for a rabble-rouser named Richard Parker. Parker had, by all accounts, once been a naval officer. What is certain is that he had been twice discharged from the service. On the first occasion, he had insulted his commanding officer: on the second, the ship's surgeon had suggested that he was going out of his mind. However, the presters showed small sense of discrimination. Shortly after Parker had been let out of prison after serving a sentence for debt, they rounded him up and inflicted him on the long suffering Navy for a third time.

Richard Parker, one of the leaders of the Nore mutiny in 1797, presents a list of grievances to Vice Admiral Buckner. The revolt failed and Parker and about thirty others were hanged.

Richard Parker, who was now languishing at the Nore in a receiving ship named HMS *Sandwich*, clearly had at least one talent. He was a born demagogue. He had a fine flow of rhetoric, and a consuming sense of his own importance. Had he been at Spithead, the mutiny would have been the very stuff of life to him. As things were, and having noted the success of the Spithead affair, he sat down to compose his own set of demands. The *Sandwich* was a good place to begin: it was crammed with malcontents and the conditions were appalling. Parker and some kindred spirits overcame the officers and hoisted a red flag. This very mixed-up seaman now proclaimed himself "President of the Floating Republic." When the admiral commanding at the Nore refused the terms, the mutiny spread to Yarmouth, where Admiral Duncan was in charge. Duncan was a large character of considerable strength. While Parker was making plans to blockade the Port of London, Duncan was dealing with matters in his own way. He picked up the mutineers' local ringleader, and threatened to throw him overboard. A few days later, it all fizzled out and Parker surrendered.

Admiral Duncan sailed away with his fleet; met the Dutch fleet in the North Sea; and gave them a thorough trouncing off their own coast at Camperdown. Parker and about thirty other mutineers were hanged. At

Opposite. Cruel officers could make a seaman's life a misery. Young midshipmen, often cheeky and up to sly tricks, were among the most unpopular.

the last moment, he seems to have regretted his role, for he wrote: "Remember never to make yourself the busybody of the lower classes for they are cowardly, selfish and ungrateful; the least trifle will intimidate them, and him whom they have exalted one moment as their Demagogue, the next they will not scruple to exalt upon the gallows. I own it is with pain that I make such a remark to you, but truth demands it. I have experimentally proved it, and am very soon to be made an example of it."

Surprisingly, the mutinies at Spithead and the Nore had nothing to do with the cruelty of officers, or the impressment of sailors. In both cases, there would have been ample justification. Nor, indeed, was the question of prize money raised. There certainly was cause for dissension; but – surprisingly, perhaps – the agitators overlooked it. While the officers were raking it in at the rate of, perhaps, one thousand pounds, a seaman's share was a mere guinea (i.e. £1.05).

Brutality, of course, depended on the nature of the officers. There were what the lower deck called "taut hands" – captains, in other words, who were the very devil. Nor were some of their underlings much better. Jack Nastyface – the pen-name of a seaman named William Robinson, whose memoirs provide the best account of lowerdeck life in Nelson's time – had this to say about a midshipman: "We had a mid-shipman on board our

A frequent complaint of the seamen, as this cartoon shows, was that they did not receive a fair share of prize money. Most went to the officers.

ship of a wickedly mischievous disposition, whose sole delight was to insult the feelings of the seamen, and furnish pretexts to get them punished. His conduct made every man's life miserable that happened to be under his orders. He was a youth not more than twelve or thirteen years of age; but I have often seen him get on the carriage of a gun, call a man to him, and kick him about the thighs and body, and with his fist would beat him about the head; and these, although prime seamen, at the same time dared not murmur." This particular youngster was later killed in action. Wrote Nastyface, ". . . when it was known that he was killed, the general exclamation was, '*Thank God, we are rid of the young tyrant!*' His death was hailed as the triumph over an enemy." The moral, he believed, should not go unremarked by other officers.

Brutal Punishment

Flogging was either a casual affair or a ceremonial. There were the canes of the boatswains and the lieutenants which made the seaman's life a painful burden when carrying out his day-to-day duties. Some of the more villainous boatswains used a rope's end, which hurt even more and sometimes resulted in injury. An officer who had accompanied Captain Cook in his voyage around the world, wrote to the head of the Admiralty: "I served in a ship where every one of the main topmen were stripped and

Below. Naval justice was harsh and senior officers could sometimes suffer as well as the crew. Admiral Byng was shot in 1757 for failing to relieve Minorca.

For the ordinary seamen even small offences could be punished with great brutality. This man has been tied to the rigging and is being lashed in front of the crew as a warning to them not to disobey orders.

flogged for no other cause than that another ship in the company got her topgallant yards up first, and not for any wilful negligence on the part of the men. Had we been first, possibly the topmen of the other ship might have been the sufferers."

Few accounts of floggings fully convey the horror and brutality of the punishment. For example, a sailor named John noted: "Thomas Breedon received his thirty-six lashes. All hands were sorry for him but it is no use commenting on the faults of others but I hope I shall never see such another sight. Although he never murmured the twitching of every lash told that he must have felt it acutely for he is a very fleshy man." Later in the year, when two seamen named Ramsay and Reynolds each received forty-eight lashes, he observed that "both took it very well. Reynolds groaned a little but Ramsey never uttered a murmur. I say why not flog an officer as well as a man. If it teaches a lesson to men why not an officer? What is good for the goose is surely good for the gander?"

Punishments for more serious offences had to be seen to take place. Doubtless, the purpose was to discourage other men from committing them. Let Jack Nastyface take up the story: "About eleven o'clock, or six bells, when any of the men are in irons, or on the black list, the boatswain or mate are ordered to call all hands; the culprits are then brought forward by the master at arms, who is a warrant officer . . . he likewise has the prisoners in his custody, until they are put in irons, under any charge.

Life on board was easier for the officers. Their accommodation was less cramped and their food, and especially drink, was much better than that of the crew.

All hands being now mustered, the captain orders the man to strip; he is then seized to a grating by the wrists and knees; his crime is then mentioned, and the prisoner may plead, but, in nineteen cases out of twenty, he is flogged for the most trifling offence or neglect, such as not hearing the watch called out at night, not doing anything properly on deck or aloft, which he might happen to be sent to do, when, perhaps he has been doing the best he could. . . ."

The ultimate penalty was, of course, to be hanged from a yardarm. It was reserved for mutiny and murder. One of the more practised exponents of supervising these grim occasions was Lord St. Vincent. "What," he once asked his secretary, "do they [the Admiralty] think I am, that they ask me to perform the duties of a common hangman?" In all fairness to His Lordship, he disliked the role intensely; and was, in fact, extremely popular with his men.

Nowadays, the penal code at sea appears to have achieved a degree of brutality that knew hardly any limits. To contemporary observers, however, it doubtless seemed less harsh. People were accustomed to this sort of thing, and punishment meted out to sailors was no more severe than that received by offenders on shore. At one time, a criminal could be hanged for stealing anything worth a shilling (5p.) or more, and a man counted himself fortunate if he was sentenced to transportation. Nor was there any discrimination so far as age was concerned. In the eighteenth

Opposite. A new volunteer for the navy signs on. His lot would be poor pay, bad rations and brutal discipline.

century, children shared the gallows with their elders. Justice was entirely blind: before uttering his verdict, a judge was likely to ask: "Have you anything to say before I hang you?" The most the villain could answer was "Good bye"!

After witnessing the ordeals of their companions, the men were treated to what was probably the most popular moment of the day. At noon, a musician used to play *Nancy Dawson* on a fife, and the hands received their issue of grog – which was followed by the midday meal. From Nastyface: "It is the duty of the cook from each mess to fetch and serve it to his messmates, of which every man and boy is allowed a pint, that is, one gill of rum and three of water, to which is added lemon acid [the Admiralty had at last learned the lemon juice lesson from the East India Company], sweetened with sugar. Here I must remark, that the cook comes in for the perquisites of office, by reserving to himself an extra portion of grog, which is called the over-plus, and generally comes to the double of a man's allowance. . . . It may be known to every one that it is grog which pays debts, and not money, in a man of war."

Meanwhile, on shore, the press gang went about its duties. It was estimated that it cost £20 to impress a man into the Navy, of which the men responsible received £5. The captains of ships also had a duty in this respect. In 1803, the Admiral at Torquay issued an order that each captain should "select from the crew of his Majesty's ship under your command a sufficient number of trusty and well disposed men to man three boats, with as many marines and petty officers as you may judge necessary to send in each, under the orders of a lieutenant, to whom you will deliver a press warrant. . . . And you are likewise to select sixteen steady marines that may be trusted to go on shore to stop the avenues leading up to the country. . . .

"You will endeavour to have previous communication with one of His Majesty's Justices of the Peace for the district, applying to him to back the warrants, taking especial care to cause as little alarm as possible. On the boats returning to the ships, you will make a return to me of the number and qualities of the men that you may have impressed. . . ."

Press gangs were usually led by men who had been naval officers. They were armed with clubs and paid on a type of commission basis.

Once a man was on board ship during the Napoleonic Wars, he remained there. Shore leave was granted only on rare occasions, and then only for compassionate reasons. If a man decided to disobey the rule, he did so at his peril. Landsmen were rewarded handsomely for any deserting mariners they turned over to the authorities, and there was hardly anyone the sailor could trust. In 1810, four impressed men tried to make a break for it. They were captured and sentenced to be "flogged through the fleet" – in other words, given twenty-five lashes from a cat-o'-nine-tails at each ship. As one of the men said when he heard the verdict, "I am sure I cannot go through the torture; I would rather have been sentenced to be shot, or hung at the yardarm." Faced with such possibilities, most of the mariners took the prudent action of remaining on board: though some must have recalled a remark by Dr. Johnson that "No man would be a sailor who has contrivance enough to get himself into a jail; for being in a ship is being in a jail, with the chance of being drowned. A man in jail has more room, better food and commonly better company."

Even if their ship was in port, sailors were seldom allowed shore leave. However, to make their leisure more tolerable, women were allowed on board. *Right.* Women being rowed out to the ships and, *opposite,* on board.

Life in Port

Admittedly, the authorities made a spell in port as pleasant as possible. On Sunday afternoons, the men were allowed to visit other ships. Women were permitted on board. Local boatmen used to charge seven shillings (35p.) each to row them out to the vessels – on the strict understanding that no money would be handed over if, at the end of the trip, their passengers had not found sailors who would accept them.

Some of the officers carried out a process of selection before the local talent was allowed up the gangway. These lieutenants were jealous of their ships' reputations, and they would only allow attractive and well-dressed ladies on board. The raddled shrews were sent smartly back to the shore; but the boatmen soon realized who would and who would not be acceptable. Many of them used to make five pounds a day from this traffic.

As for the girls, most of them remained on the ship until she was ready to put to sea once more. Some of them changed hands several times during their spell on board. Others pretended to be married to the men who had claimed them. There was no privacy, but nobody seemed to mind. On many occasions, there were no fewer than five hundred women in a ship at the same time.

The busy scene at Portsmouth Point when the fleet was in port. By Thomas Rowlandson.

SHIP
TAVERN

When the ships left port some of the women on board were allowed to stay for the voyage. The theory seems to have been that a little sex helped a man to relax after a battle. Certainly women helped to nurse the wounded. During the Battle of the Nile in 1798 a woman from Edinburgh gave birth to a boy in HMS *Goliath*.

One would have to be very innocent indeed, however, to imagine that the majority of the ladies flocked to the men-of-war for love. There had to be some more tangible rewards. But, whatever their cupidity, it was nothing when compared to that of a segment of society known, unjustly and not without racial prejudice, as "the Jews." These gentlemen, who combined the roles of salesmen and money lenders, used to swarm aboard a man-of-war as soon as she had come to anchor. Since the sailors were not paid immediately, many of the Jews would advance them sums of cash. A fair proportion of these debts were never repaid; but, to quote Captain Marryat, "the Jews' charges were so extravagant that if one-third of their bills were paid there still remained a profit." Later on, to protect the men, these economic vultures were not allowed on board until pay-day – usually a day or two before the ship sailed again.

Their merchandise covered a wide field, from "gold" watches which only kept going for a week – to way-out uniforms that were much more colourful than the versions sold by the purser;* from brass telescopes to scarlet handkerchiefs; straw hats and crockery, spoons and sheath knives, clay pipes and Dutch cheeses. The prices charged were, on average, about five times those one would expect to pay on shore. Not unnaturally, the sailors suspected they were being cheated, and fights often broke out.

Girls and the "Jews" were tolerated in port: drink was forbidden. Nevertheless, the sailors managed to smuggle it aboard. The popular tipple was known as "red-eye." Gin, and a concoction called "sailor's joy" were also available. It would be hard to say which, out of this unholy

Ibbetson, the artist who painted this picture, described it as "the jolly tars of Old England on a land cruise."

* There was no official uniform for naval ratings until 1857.

The ship's cook. Many of these men had wooden legs, which made them unfit for other duties.

trio, was the most lethal. But the mariners and the salesmen exercised considerable ingenuity in getting it past the gimlet eyes of the master-at-arms. Cocoa-nut shells, balls of lard, oranges, scent bottles and sheep's bladders were among the devices adapted to conceal it.

Pay day took place as the vessel was being got ready for sea. "In the early part of the day," Jack Nastyface wrote, "the commissioners came on board, bringing the money which is paid to the ship's crew, with the exception of six months pay, which it is the rule of the government to hold back from each man. The mode of paying is, as the names are, by rotation on the books: every man, when called, is asked for his hat, which is returned to him with his wages in it, and the amount chalked on the rim. There is not perhaps one in twenty who actually knows what he is going to receive, nor does the particular amount seem to be a matter of much concern; for, when paid, they hurry down to their respective berths, redeem their honour with their several ladies and bomb-boat* men, and then they turn their thoughts to the Jew pedlars, who are ranged round the decks and in the hatchway gratings, in fact, the ship is crowded with them."

Shanties

Just as in the merchant service, tasks on naval vessels were performed to a rhythm. The difference was that, whilst the merchant seamen sang shanties, these songs were forbidden in men-of-war. Instead, the men's labours were accompanied by a fiddle or a fife, or simply by calling out

Gunners moving a carronade into the firing position.

* Bomb boat: more commonly known as bum-boat. It was used to carry provisions and generally to act as a link with the shore. So-called from "bombard" – a vessel in which beer was carried to soldiers on duty.

Whether on board a warship or a merchantman, the officers lived very well. The bewigged dog shows the artist William Hogarth's view of such a contrast with the lives of the crews.

numbers. And, even in merchant ships, the art of the shanty went into a decline during the Napoleonic wars. Most of the vessels had guns mounted on them, and their crews became infected by naval customs. When returning to Britain, the presence of the inevitable press gang tender made the occasion scarcely one for song. Furthermore, after a while, most of the good shantymen had been pressed into the Navy. As Stan Hugill writes in *Shanties from the Seven Seas*, "Obviously shantying *did* exist, but only as a trickle; and even mention of this trickle has been omitted from the nautical works of this period."

The Quality of Seamen

One sometimes has the impression that British seamen suffered more from their superiors during the Napoleonic Wars, than they did from the French. Nevertheless, they comprised the finest maritime fighting force in the world. Some of them were, admittedly, taken from the dregs of society. Once a criminal on shore had been convicted, nothing could save him from his fate. But, if he volunteered or was pressed into service before coming to trial, he was likely to escape the grim sentence of the judge. The fact that he might be committing himself to a world which was hardly less brutal did not seem to occur to him. Even French prisoners-of-war sometimes fought against their own countrymen by joining the Royal Navy. In these instances, they responded to offers of what passed for freedom – provided they volunteered.

These men were knocked into some sort of shape by the harsh discipline on shipboard. It may have been a great character-builder: it was certainly a deterrent. Furthermore, it would be wrong to consider that the Royal Navy of the period was manned by the dregs of the earth. Far from it: the backbone of the service were men who had joined willingly – accomplished seamen, staunchly loyal to the service, and proud of the ships in which they worked. Nelson was particularly aware of this. His opinion of his vessels was not very high; but he had a great admiration for the men who sailed them. When his Mediterranean squadron was given the task of blockading Toulon, he wrote: "I never saw a fleet so well officered and manned. Would to God the ships were half as good! . . . My crazy ships are getting into a very indifferent state, and others will soon follow. The finest ones in service would soon be destroyed by such terrible weather. I know well enough that if I were to go into Malta, I should save the ships during this bad season. But if I am to watch the French, I must be at sea; and if at sea, must have bad weather. And if the ships are not fit to stand bad weather, they are useless. Unfortunately in bad weather I am always seasick."

Nelson was very concerned about finding a "mode of inducing the Seamen to be fond, and even desirous, of serving in the Navy, in preference to the Merchant Service." He believed that "their pay and provisions cannot possibly be improved from what they are at present;" but he was always at pains to see that they actually received them. In 1797, having covered himself with glory at the Battle of Cape St. Vincent, he transferred from the *Captain* to the *Theseus*. Morale in his new vessel, as he quickly discovered, was very low indeed. The reason was that the stores had become exhausted, and nobody had done anything about replenishing them. He set about making good the deficiency. Within a week, the men had all they needed.

Sailors worshipped Nelson. Jack Nastyface, whose view of officers was by no means uncritical, refers to him as "my noble and ever to be lamented brave commander." The sailors in HMS *Theseus* sent him a note, saying: "Success attend Admiral Nelson. God bless Captain Miller.

A sailor went off on his first voyage as a callow boy . . . and returned as a man. "The Sailor's Farewell" and "The Sailor's Return" by C. Mosley (1744).

Lord Nelson (*above*) was born in 1789, the same year that his future flagship H.M.S. *Victory* was laid-down. Although Nelson was loved by his sailors, there is no reason to believe that his discipline was less harsh than that of his contemporaries. But he did try to ensure that his men were adequately fed.

Nelson, even as a young officer, never lacked courage. Here he is setting out to board a prize. Artist's impression.

We thank them for the officers they have placed over us. We are happy and comfortable, and will shed every drop of blood in our veins, and the name of the *Theseus* shall be immortalised as high as the *Captain*'s." These were the words of the men who, a week previously, had been on the verge of mutiny; and whose apparently much-loved Captain Miller had often ordered no fewer than forty-eight lashes for a single offence.

And, from the crew of *Foudroyant*'s barge, after the Admiral had transferred his flag to another ship: "My Lord: It is with extreme grief that we find you are about to leave us. We have been with you . . . in every engagement Your Lordship has been in, both by Sea and Land; and most humbly beg of Your Lordship to permit us to go to England as your Boats Crew, in any Ship or Vessel that may seem most pleasing to Your Lordship. My Lord, pardon the rude Style of Seamen, who are but little acquainted with writing, and believe us to be, My Lord, your ever humble and obedient servents. . . ."

But it all came to an end at Trafalgar. So far as this book is concerned, let the story of that battle be told by a letter from a seaman to his father. "When the game began," he wrote, "I wished myself back with the plough again, but when they had given us one duster [i.e. fired on them], and I found myself snug and tight, I set to in good earnest, and thought no more about being killed than if I were at Murrell Green Fair, and I was presently as busy and black as a collier. How my [three] fingers got knocked overboard I don't know, but off they are, and I never missed them till I wanted them. . . . We have taken a rare parcel of ships, but the wind is so rough we cannot bring them home, else I should roll in money, so we are busy smashing 'em, and blowing them up wholesale.

"Our dear Admiral Nelson is killed, so we have paid pretty sharply for licking them. I never set eyes on him, for which I am both sorry and glad; for, to be sure, I should like to have seen him – but then, all the men in our ship who have seen him are such soft toads, they have done nothing but blast their eyes, and cry, ever since he was killed. God bless you! Chaps that fought like the devil, sit down and cry like a wench."

The preoccupations of war were such that nobody paid very much attention to a small vessel which, in 1802, began her trials on the River Clyde. Her name was the *Charlotte Dundas*. Towing two fully laden barges, she managed to travel into the face of a strong wind at a speed of three knots. HMS *Victory*, a thirty-four year old veteran sailing ship when Nelson was on board her at Trafalgar, was the shape of the past. The *Charlotte Dundas* was a symbol of the future. She was a steamship.

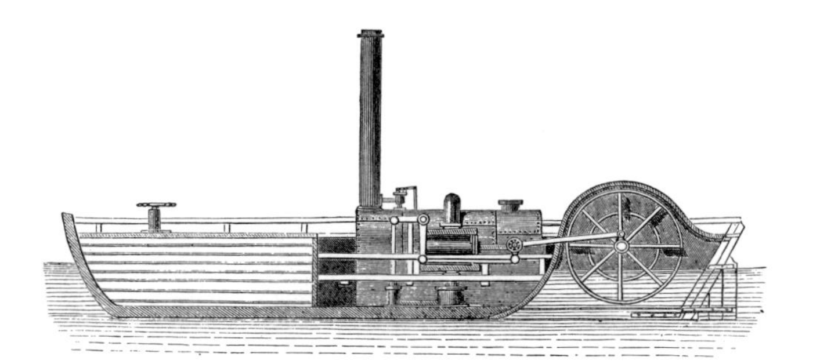

Opposite. The French and British battle fleets locked in combat at the Battle of Trafalgar.

Left. Shipping's new face: the *Charlotte Dundas*, a steam boat which, in 1802, towed two laden barges into a strong wind at the rate of three knots.

5 *Whisps of Smoke*

The last battle to be fought exclusively by sailing ships took place in the Bay of Navarino, off Greece, in 1827, when a force commanded by Admiral Sir Edward Codrington smashed a combined Turkish and Egyptian fleet. Although there were a great many naval officers who thought – and, possibly, hoped – to the contrary, sail was on its way out. But, then, these gentlemen were renowned for their conservatism. In the year before Navarino, a writer on naval affairs had observed: "The old school of seamen consisted, and still consists of the most prejudiced beings in existence; nothing novel, in their opinion, was or is, either safe or available. They revered with a spice of idolatry everything on the old plan, however tardy the process, or cumbrous the machinery. . . ."

Charlotte Dundas's trials on the River Clyde had been by no means the first experiments with steam as a method of ship propulsion. Back in 1794, the Earl of Stanhope had become preoccupied with the idea. In his eagerness to convince the Admiralty that here, at last, was the answer to adverse winds and the impossibility of manoeuvring in still weather, he had built an experimental vessel named the *Kent*. But, before the project began, he had been compelled to guarantee £9,000 – for the purpose of indemnifying "the public in case the said ship should not answer the purpose of the government." It was just as well. The *Kent* spent most of her brief life in a dock adjacent to the River Thames. The experiment was deemed to be a failure.

But not all ventures into the world of steam fared so badly. By 1824, progress had reached a point at which it was possible to offer a prize of £8,000 for the first steamship to reach India within a specified time. A Deptford-built 470-ton vessel named the *Enterprise* made the passage in 113 days. The details of the exploit are vague. The donor of the reward is unknown, and there is some doubt about how much time the *Enterprise* spent steaming, and how much sailing. One account suggests that her engines were used for 103 out of the 113 days: another, that they were employed for only 63 days. But there seems to be no doubt that she spent 10½ days taking on coal.

The important thing was that she had accomplished the voyage. Shortly afterwards, another steamer, the *Falcon*, travelled to Calcutta as a speculative venture. Her builders had hoped to sell her to the Indian Government. They were disappointed. Nobody wanted this new-fangled toy.

Opposite. The steamships *Sirius* (*left*) and *Great Western* (*right*) in New York harbour, 1838. A berth on an America-bound steamer was the best a sailor could hope for. The pay was better than on east-bound ships – and the voyage shorter.

The Battle of Navarino, 1827, was the last naval combat fought exclusively by sailing ships.

The Admiralty was not as quick as the merchant navies to take advantage of a form of power which made ships independent of the wind. They feared the effect of shells on the exposed paddle wheels, and insisted that steamships should only be used for towing men-of-war in and out of harbour.

A cartoonist's view (published 1835) of the fitting out of a young officer recruit at the start of his naval career.

Taking Steam Seriously

However, there were those in Britain who took steam seriously. The main objection to it, from the point of view of the merchant fleet, was cost. After all, wind is free: coal has to be bought. It appeared to be a viable proposition for the mails and passengers, but its role for cargo carriers was doubtful. It would be possible to send letters to India more quickly by this method: provided there were sufficient people prepared to pay one shilling in excess of the normal postage, and provided each communication did not weigh more than half-an-ounce. In some respects, it was rather like air mail. As for the passengers: the fares would be substantially higher, and the traffic would be limited to rich business men and officials in a hurry. For such lowly characters as emigrants, sailing ships would have to do – just as they would have to serve for any other commodity in large quantities.

The Navy was in no eagerness to adopt steam engines for its warships. It would, the majority of senior officers agreed, be all right for tugboats and packet boats, but hardly the thing for a man-of-war. As Lord Melville wrote to Brunel: "The Board deem it unnecessary to enter at present into a consideration of the question as to how far the steam-engine may be made applicable to the general purposes of navigation, but as it would be attended with material advantages to His Majesty's service if it could be used for towing ships out of harbour in the Thames or Medway, and at Portsmouth and Plymouth, when they would be prevented from sailing by contrary winds, desire him to submit his ideas on that part of the subject, if it appears to him to be practicable."

Admiralty indifference to the new source of power did not spring entirely from the reactionary sentiments of its officers. There were many good reasons why it might serve for tugs and, even, large merchantmen, but not for ships-of-war. The only available means of propulsion was the paddle-wheel, which would be extremely vulnerable to gunfire. Nor,

If a sailor got drunk, he ended up in the irons. But this was the least of his troubles, for flogging almost inevitably followed.

Steamships had a very important advantage over sail – they rode rough water very much better. The P & O steamship *Jupiter*.

encased in a wooden hull, were the engines likely to fare very much better in battle. Much more work would have to be done on the development of the screw; and iron ships (which Their Lordships opposed with even more vigour – but that is another story) would have to be built, before sails could be dispensed with.

But there were those who kept on trying. From Sir John Barrow, Secretary of the Admiralty to Lord Melbourne: "There had been a steamship . . . called the *Regent* . . . purchased as a packet to run from Margate to London. He [I. K. Brunel] says: 'On 9th July, 1816, the *Regent* left Margate with a strong gale of wind blowing right ahead, and against a very strong tide. When out at sea the gale increased very much and the sea broke over the vessel for several hours. The covering of the wheels was stove in; they, however, received no injury, though they were now and then overwhelmed. The steam-engine yielding gradually and for a moment to a greater power was soon in action again.'"

Such evidence was not to be ignored. In 1823, the Navy took possession of its first steamship, HMS *Lightening* – a tugboat. She came into service two years after the first regular steam cross-channel service had been introduced. By 1826, two engineers had been in charge of her. The current incumbent was a gentleman named John Chapender. One of Mr. Chapender's reports shows something of his life – and, albeit unwittingly, reveals himself. "I should [he tells the Chief Engineer of Portsmouth Dockyard] have wrote to you before of our arrival at Deptford but I have been so bussey imployed in towing ships about that I have not had an hour since I left Cronstead in Rusia we left it on the 1 of July in company with the *Couester* 74 [guns] after beatin and towing her

Sailors liked working on the packet boats across the English Channel, as it meant they saw their families more often. Passengers, however, found it less enjoyable.

at time we was ten days and nights before we made Copheagen after working that time my water in the boilers did not exceed the tempeture of 216 Deg. by blowing some water from the boilers several times a day. We took our departure from Copheagen on the 13th inst. and then went into a port in Norway in a gale of wind on the 17 inst. at this place Biggs departed on 19 Inst this life and was buried their the tempeture of the boilers did not exceed 216 Deg. . . ." And so on.

As Mr. Chapender's report may suggest, he was not a very well educated man; but he was reasonably typical. Some naval officers used to refer to the early marine engineers as "Engine Drivers." The remark was intended to be disparaging: in many cases, however, it was the precise truth. Some of them had, indeed, gone to sea from the footplates of railway locomotives.

The executive officers' relations with the engineers were uneasy and, sometimes, comical. In *The Navy as I have Known It*, Admiral the Hon. Sir Edmund Fremantle recalled conditions on board HMS *Salamander*. "From the bridge of the *Salamander*," Sir Edmund wrote, "one could see the steam gauge, and if the steam was up to its proper pressure it should have

Although the Royal Navy acquired its first steamship in 1823, as late as 1860 her sailors were still being trained to man *sailing* ships.

marked 7 lbs. . . . The Chief Engineer's name was Hoggs, and the Commander's Eltham. They did not get on well together, and I often heard the following dialogue, the difficulty of aspiration being about equally divided between the two officers.

"The Commander would look down, and seeing the steam gauge up to 4 or 6 lbs. only, would call out 'Keep the steam up, Mr. 'Oggs!' the answer coming promptly, in an annoying tone from the engine room 'Hall right, Captain Helltham.' "

One commander, Captain Hugh Pigott of HMS *Barham*, found himself before a court martial in 1834 for ordering a junior officer to flog a chief engineer. He had refused on the grounds that "[I] stated that I could not flog Harris, he being a petty, if not a warrant, officer and Chief

Engineer, there being an order issued at the time His Majesty was Lord High Admiral, forbidding future infliction of corporal punishment upon petty officers. Captain Pigott then ordered me to disrate him, to which I replied that I did not think that I had the power to do so, as he had been appointed by the Navy Board. He asked to see this appointment, which upon enquiry, could not be found. When I informed Captain Pigott of this he said that Harris could not be recognized as a warrant or petty officer, and that I might flog him."

It had a happy ending – of a kind. Harris was neither flogged nor disrated; and the court martial acquitted Captain Pigott on a number of charges which included "oppressive conduct and endangering his ship." Furthermore, Pigott had established a useful precedent. No matter how much their commanding officers might disapprove of them and their machinery, engineers were entitled to a certain status. The argument that sailors drove a vessel by tending the sails could not be applied to these technicians. They were experts after a fashion, and not to be strung up and scourged whenever they created a misdemeanour. They had, in a word, *rank*.

When, in 1837, naval engineers became established, they were appointed by Admiralty Warrant (as opposed to deck officers, who held the Royal Commission). In the social structure of a ship, they ranked below the carpenter, but just above the cook – who was a petty officer. In 1846, the Admiralty announced its intention to raise them from warrant officers to commissioned officers. Predictably, it aroused a storm of protest. Typical was this letter, which appeared in *The Times* under the signature of "Wardroom:" "I have, with some surprise, read a paragraph in *The Times* of 20 Inst., in which it is stated to be the intention of the Admiralty to make engineers of Her Majesty's Navy commissioned officers and that they are to mess with the Lieutenants etc. . . . Now without in the slightest degree wishing to say anything against that class of officers, I believe I am speaking the sentiments of every officer in the navy when I say that such a step as that proposed in *The Times* would not only give dissatisfaction, but would be prejudicial at the same time to the service in general; and I believe firmly that the engineers themselves would be against anything of the sort. They would feel themselves placed in a position they were not intended to fill – among a superior class of people altogether, and by whom, generally speaking, they would be looked down upon as out of their station in society. . . ."

The engineers were not the only ones who were mistrusted: anybody with technical pretentions came under suspicion. Gunnery, for example, had been a very inexact science. The art, it was believed, lay in making as many bangs as possible in a brief time. The fact that a good many might fall wide of the mark did not seem to bother anybody. What, they implied, had been good enough for Nelson was good enough for everyone else.

However, in the mid-1830s, a fresh generation of naval officers was growing up: young men, that is to say, who were not old enough to have experienced the tactics of Trafalgar, and who were inclined to question the old methods. When confronted with their ideas, their superiors took refuge in ignorance – real or pretended. On one occasion, a Naval Lord named Sir Charles Rowley was looking at some examination papers by lieutenants who had recently completed a course in gunnery. At some point, Sir Charles exclaimed, "Do you know, it is very strange, but I don't understand all this. Pray, sir, what is the meaning of the word 'impact'?"

On being told that "I rather think it means the force of a blow," Sir Charles turned to a colleague (Sir John Poo Beresford), and asked: "What, in the name of good fortune is meant by 'initial velocity'?"

Sir John said: "I'll be hanged if I know, but I rather think it is some of [that] scientific bosh."

The Merchant service was quicker to recognize the possibilities of steam. In the first half of the nineteenth century, there were only a few large shipping companies.* Most of the tonnage was owned by small outfits – some of them syndicates in which the master of the vessel had a stake. The older established firms experimented cautiously with steamships, but took pains to keep their fleets of sailing vessels up-to-date. A few were more adventurous. Among the pioneers was a firm of stage-coach owners in Dublin. The name of the enterprise was Messrs. Bourne.

Messrs. Bourne had a contract for transporting the mails in Ireland. In this capacity, they became the main proprietors of the Dublin and London Steam Packet Company – a progressive undertaking, which had been one of the first shipping companies to employ steam engines. One of their ships was a steamer named *Royal Tar*. Through London shipbrokers, they had chartered the *Royal Tar* to the Spanish Government. The small "puffer" was so successful that, before very long, the Spanish Ambassador was in touch with Messrs. Bourne. Would they, he wanted to know, consider running a steamship service to Spain? In this manner, the P. & O. line came about. Its original name was the Peninsular Steam Navigation Company. Nowadays the initials stand for Peninsular and Orient.

By 1838, the North Atlantic had two steamers (the *Great Western* and the *Sirius*) running a regular service across it. In 1840, a gentleman from

"The Irish Packet entering the Mersey, 1831," a painting by Samuel Walters. One of the first companies to see the profit to lie in regular steamship services was a firm of stage-coach proprietors in Dublin.

* A situation which was changed by the passing of the Limited Liability Act in 1862, which produced that abstract entity of modern commerce – the shareholder.

Nova Scotia named Samuel Cunard established an office in Liverpool, and put four ocean greyhounds (steam-driven) on the route to North America. By 1842, the P. & O. line had stretched out its steamship service to reach India. And, by 1874, although there were still 203,606 British merchant seamen serving in sailing ships, no fewer than 74,843 were employed in steamers. Like almost everything else in the mid-nineteenth century, the shipping world was in a state of change. The idea was long obsolete that the only place in which a mariner could learn his trade was in a sailing vessel.

Black sailors worked on many English ships in the eighteenth and early nineteenth centuries. This one was a cook. *Below.* Animals were often kept live on board, such as the goats seen below, who provided milk.

The Need for Higher Standards

What effect was all this having on the men who worked the ships? A British Consul who was asked for his opinion in 1869, said: "Year by year, our merchant ships are manned by an inferior class of sailors, whose insubordination and unruliness are yearly on the increase. The masters are really almost powerless to enforce discipline; their hands are tied by law, and the seamen know it. It is but a few days since that the masters of all the British vessels in this port [St. Michael's in the Azores], some twenty in number, came to me in a body to complain of the mutinous conduct of their men."

Our man in Amsterdam observed that the crews of steamships gave "far less trouble than those of sailing vessels;" and the Consul in Smyrna was inclined to agree with him. "The crews of steamers," this official said, "belonging to the opulent companies give little or no trouble, as they are all picked men, and are much better provided for than the seamen belonging to sailing ships, which appear to be obliged to take what is refused by the steamers."

The standard of seamanship, certainly, does not appear to have been very high. Between 1856 and 1862, sixty vessels were lost at sea from defects in their construction. On the other hand, no fewer than 711 were

wrecked as the result of neglect or bad navigation.

According to the *Shipping Gazette*, "The evidence, taken for a series of years before courts of inquiry, proves unquestionably that ships have been lost by defective look-out, by negligent or ignorant steering, and by the want of seamanlike skill and knowledge among their crews; but the evidence proves also that the ships have been lost by recklessness, ignorance, neglect, or incompetence on the part of masters and officers, and especially of the latter."

Better things might have been expected of the officers. In 1850, the Navigation Act was repealed. In its place was passed *An Act for Improving the conditions of Masters, Mates and Seamen and maintaining Discipline in the Merchant Service*. It stipulated that a Marine Department should be set up at the Board of Trade, with responsibility for shipping. It became obligatory to keep a log book. Marine Boards were set up at principal seaports to examine the seaworthiness of vessels. The accommodation for the crews was to be improved; and, most important of all, officers now had to hold certificates of efficiency. Later, this was extended to engineers.

The *Shipping Gazette* had been one of the earliest advocates of a system of examinations for masters and mates. Since the Act had come into force in 1850, how could the alarming shipwreck statistics be accounted for? Might not an improvement have been expected? The magazine's editorial writer contented himself with saying that "the system has not by any means completed its work, or produced the results of which, properly administered, it is capable." It was, perhaps, better to travel in hope – though the outlook was not encouraging. As if to support the *Shipping Gazette*, Sir Thomas Brassey, writing in 1877, noted that "It may be appropriate to point out that in no instance has an officer been punished, except by loss of certificate, for gross negligence, even when leading to loss of life, since the loss of the *Orion* in Scotland, more than twenty years ago."

Space on board a man of war was never wasted: even the crew's hammocks were slung so as to fit the maximum men in the smallest space.

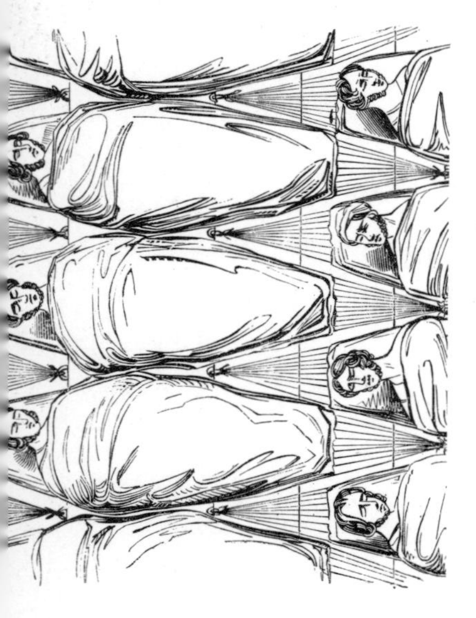

Beneath its somewhat wordy title, the new Act may have had a heart of gold. The average seaman, however, might have been forgiven if he could not see it. Little was done to improve the accommodation. Ships were undermanned and over-loaded; and the food was still appalling – usually hard tack (ship's biscuit), watery pea soup and salt pork. A story used to be told of a captain whose crew were constantly complaining about the meals. One day, his wife urged him to give them something better. He produced duck and green peas, which she herself cooked to ensure they were nicely done. When one old mariner received his helping, he promptly threw it overboard. When his companions told him that he had made a mistake, and that the dish was excellent, he replied: "They must have had something the matter with them to be cheap enough to be given to us."

One shipowner who received a request that his men's rations should include tinned milk, reacted with horror. "Milk with their tea!" he spluttered. "Why? They're not invalids."

Accommodation Fit for Animals

Accommodation for the crew was up front in the forecastle. Describing the amenities as they were towards the end of the nineteenth century,

A medieval fleet transporting soldiers to war.

Cook landing at Mallicolo, later renamed the New Hebrides, in July 1774. Such voyages widened the seamen's experience: they saw many strange sights and visited lands that had been little more than myths before.

Four members of a ship's crew painted by Thomas Rowlandson in 1799: (*left*) the purser, (*below left*) the carpenter, (*above*) a sailor, (*below*) a cabin boy.

Life for the ordinary seamen in the early nineteenth century. The accommodation was neither spacious nor comfortable.

Overleaf. A Sunday morning service on board a warship serving in the Baltic fleet, 1855.

Dr. W. E. Home recalled that it was "a wedge-shaped space. . . . This is divided by a central partition, and the sailors live on the starboard side, stokers on the port side. It is some six feet six inches high, and is built of iron beams over which are spread iron plates. The space for twelve sailors would be 864 cubic feet or less (a third-class railway compartment is about 266 cubic feet, 864 is two thirds and a first) and 144 square feet of deck-space. Iron wall outside, iron partition inside. Through the space will run the spindle of the capstan and the clumsy hawse pipe, the size of a man; the encumbrances make cleaning difficult. The place will be painted yellow for cheapness and the space will be dark because the windows are so small. Then there are the berths, twelve of them, probably of wood, arranged in pairs (even threes!) one above another in six or seven feet of height, to right and left. They are ordinary bed-places of wood with a 'leeboard' to each to keep the individual from falling out. What light from the small window the upper bed does not catch is caught by the leeboard, and none ever reaches the deck, which is constantly damp and dirty. . . ."

Unless the men brought their own beds, they were provided with palliasses stuffed with straw or husks. In spite of what the British Consul at St. Michael's may have imagined, discipline was harsh, and the men worked an eighty-four hour week. Furthermore, many of the old wooden vessels were unseaworthy, and earned the name "coffin ships." If they went down with their cargoes, the owner was not particularly worried. There was always the insurance. . . .

One ally of the mariners, who became known as "the Sailor's Friend," was Samuel Plimsoll. In 1851, he had been secretary of the Great Exhibition. Two years later, he set up in business as a coal merchant; and, between 1868 and 1880, he served as a radical MP for Derby. He was particularly concerned with the Merchant Shipping Act of 1874, which was another attempt to improve the safety and conditions of

Breakfast for the young midshipmen on board H.M.S. *Caesar* serving with the Baltic fleet in 1856. The roomy cabin and sailors to wait on the officers are in marked contrast to the crew's quarters.

seafaring. When it was passed, it featured Plimsoll's own contribution: a mark on the sides of vessels, showing what, in the opinion of the Board of Trade, was the greatest depth to which they could safely be loaded.

Exit the Press Gang and Flogging

After the Napoleonic Wars, the press gang virtually died of inactivity. The cat-of-nine-tails, on the other hand, took a long time to disappear. It was almost as if this instrument of torture were a fetish which the older officers could not bring themselves to forego. The Admiralty, to its credit, made an attempt to abolish it – or, at least, to restrain its use. In 1830, Their Lordships urged commanding officers to exercise "a safe forebearance," and made chastisement amounting to more than two dozen lashes illegal without a trial. They also demanded quarterly returns of all floggings – from 1853 onwards, these were submitted to Parliament.

Nevertheless, as an officer in HMS *Albion* wrote in 1852, "A week rarely passed without some man receiving his three or four dozen lashes at the gangway. The first time I witnessed corporal punishment I was horror-struck and, after the first minute or so, averted my eyes to avoid the ghastly sight; but after a time I became so used to seeing what was called 'scratching a man's back' that I could contemplate the spectacle from beginning to end without shrinking. The punishment of flogging was

Flogging, an all too common punishment, was carried out in front of the entire crew. This was meant to ensure good discipline.

usually inflicted for crimes of insubordination or drunkenness, more often for the latter than for the former."

And, from another writer: "The young and plucky used to consider it a feather in their caps to be able to undergo a flogging without uttering a cry, and advanced themselves considerably in the estimation of their shipmates if they took their 'four bag' like a man."

However, even the cat died in the end. In 1871, this form of punishment was "suspended in peacetime." Four years later, it was "suspended in wartime." Since it no longer appears in Queen's Regulations, we have to assume that it has vanished without trace. Nevertheless, writing in 1968, Christopher Lloyd, the late Professor of History at the Royal Naval College Greenwich, observed that flogging "was never formally abolished."

"The Sailor's Friend," the M.P. Samuel Plimsoll. By establishing a loading mark for ships, he saved many sailors' lives, because ships could no longer be overloaded and thus likely to sink in rough seas.

When, in 1837, the first established engineers were appointed, these newcomers were provided with uniforms. Executive officers had worn them ever since George II had introduced them in 1748. Apart from them, the only other uniformed people on board a warship were the marines. In theory, at any rate, a rating could wear whatever he liked.

But the wind of reform was reaching the lower deck. In 1857, the Admiralty at last specified a "uniform dress" for the sailors. It consisted of a blue cloth jacket and trousers; a white drill frock with a blue collar on which were three rows of white tape; a pea jacket, a black silk scarf, a black canvas hat surrounded by a ribbon bearing the ship's name in gold letters; a wide straw hat; and so on. Contrary to popular myth, the three rows of white tape were not intended to be symbolic of Nelson's victories, and the black silk scarf had nothing to do with his funeral.

In an early nineteenth century ditty, a maid disguises herself as a sailor, and steals aboard her true-love's ship. So:

> Aboard of my true love's ship I'll go,
> And brave each blowing gale;
> I'll splice, I'll tack, I'll reef, I'll row,
> And haul with him the sail:
> In jacket blue,
> And trousers, too,
> With him I'll cruise afar,
> There shall not be a smarter chap
> Aboard of a man-of-war.

The new regulations rendered the song-writer's description considerably more accurate.

6 *Vanishing Sails*

It must often have occurred to nineteenth century mariners that they were beset by two elements: the sea and their employers. From the crew's point-of-view, the best merchant ships had been those owned by the East India Company. This organization had not only pioneered the fight against scurvy. The accommodation in its vessels was of a much higher standard. As in men-of-war, it was situated in the 'tween decks, and the seamen were not crammed together in narrow, wedge-shaped, forecastles. But East Indiamen were run on the lines of warships. They carried guns, and they were much more expensive than ships owned by lesser commercial enterprises. At the end of the eighteenth century, it was estimated, the construction of one of them cost £40 a ton. By contrast, an ordinary merchant ship cost only £25 per ton.

But the East India Company was no more. One by one, its privileges had been removed until, after the Indian Mutiny in 1857, its assets were taken over by the Crown. For anyone who wished to make his living at sea, there was no longer a third choice. He had either to offer his services to the Navy or to the merchant marine.

Steam was gradually stealing the trade from sailing ships, but there remained a few cargoes for which the latter appeared to be the only means of transport. For example, somebody had the notion that it would be impossible to carry tea in steamers on the run from China. The stench from the engines, the theory went, would spoil the flavour. It was not until a merchant was brave enough to entrust this apparently sensitive freight to a steamship named *Robert Lowe* in 1863, that the myth was demolished. After that, the clippers (as the sailing ships were known) enjoyed only another eight years of supremacy in the tea trade. Many of them were then sold off to owners trading with Australia.

The credit for the invention of the clipper, incidentally, belongs to American shipbuilders. With ample supplies of soft wood at their disposal, they found they could build a cheaper vessel than their British competitors (who favoured hard wood). It was, however, not so robust. To compensate for this shortcoming, they improved the sailing qualities. Out went the rotund bows and heavy sterns of the old-timers. In their place, the American designers introduced long, lean, athletic-looking hulls, which handled magnificently and, as their graceful lines suggested, were very fast.

Britain was not slow to learn the lesson. In 1856, a shipyard at Greenock

Opposite. Before the sailing ship finally died out, the great clippers had a brief and spectacular life. Used on the tea trade-route between China and England, they were faster than any previous sailing ship.

produced a clipper named *Lord of the Isles*, which promptly beat two of the quickest American ships on the run from China to London. American rivalry finally petered out with the outbreak of the Civil War, but the competition to bring the first of the season's tea to London (and, thereby, fetch the highest prices) continued. The *Thermopylae* raced with the *Cutty Sark*; the *Lahloo* vied with the *Taitsing*; and the times were fantastic. From China to London in less than one hundred days became almost common-place.

By Way of Cape Horn

Until the Panama Canal came into operation in 1915, the route from the United Kingdom to the west coast of the two Americas was by way of Cape Horn. Cape Horn itself is an island, which sticks out like a fang about sixty miles to the south of Tierra del Fuego. The gales storm past it from the west, building up huge seas, and making danger and discomfort the inevitable portions of a Cape Horner's lot. One of the best descriptions of conditions in this wild part is provided by a veteran "square-rigger" named F. C. Hendry, who wrote under the name of "Shalimar." In *Around the Horn and Home Again* Captain Hendry gave this account: "The conditions on board during this long-drawn-out misery were such as, fortunately, sailormen of today rarely see. The vessel had a cargo of coal, and had left a Bristol Channel port loaded right down to her marks. . . . In bad weather the waves simply poured in torrents over her; for the greater part of the time she was like a half-tide rock, and the main deck was usually full of water. Life-lines had been stretched between the fore-castle and the break of the poop, but those did not always save us, for in hauling on the braces on the many occasions on which we wore round on to the other tack we would often be up to our necks in the rushing icy water, and sometimes several of us, losing our footing, would be swept writhing against the lee bulwarks. Modern sailing ships were never over-

Seamanship was one of the most dangerous of nineteenth-century occupations. Throughout the century newspapers were full of news about shipwrecks.

manned, and when a few of the crew, mostly foreigners, developed a form of malingering known as Cape Horn fever, it came very hard on the rest of us. . . .

"For the whole of one wild night – I don't think that I have ever known a wilder – we lay hove-to with only one sail set out of the twenty-five which we could carry. This was the main lower top-sail – a narrow sodden strip of canvas straining furiously at its chain sheets – which helped to steady the vessel as she lay rising, falling, and rolling in the trough of the sea. So continuously did the waves come crashing over the weather rail that it was almost impossible to pass along the main deck, and for the greater part of the night all hands were clustered on the poop. The wind shrieked from out of the south-west, making a weird din in the rigging, and bringing with it furious squalls of hail and snow. Movement along the poop was impossible. We could only hang on to the rails, wet, cold, and unutterably miserable, waiting for the hours of darkness to pass.

"The long delayed dawn came at last, revealing a blue-lipped, red-eyed, half-frozen group of suffering humanity, and with it the wind seemed to lull a little. . . . There was still too much wind for more sail to be set, but the captain considered it safe for the watch below to seek their quarters in forecastle and half-deck."

Normally, on the passage from west to east, ships made fast time, impelled by the gales. From east to west, on the other hand, rounding the Horn was very much harder. Some had to make several attempts before the wind relented and let them through. Many were damaged, and had to retire to the Falkland Islands to lick their wounds and have them mended. Some even returned to Rio or Montevideo for this purpose: the repairers on the Falkland Islands were good, but very expensive.

But, as a sailing ship captain told Alan Villiers, "I never heard of a well-found ship, properly handled, that didn't make it – unless she was a loss altogether. Remember, the losses are added up and the successful passages taken for granted.

"As for that, you could lose your ship just as easily running east in the Roaring Forties, for that was a wild zone, too. I very nearly lost the *Bengairn* down there, bound out of Newcastle, NSW, towards Valparaiso. A nasty shift of the wind knocked her on her beam ends, and the coal shifted with her. I thought I was getting a lesson in what happened to missing ships on that run where many had been lost – so many that under-writers were getting worried about the loss-rate."

Scurvy: the Constant Enemy

These, then, were the troubled waters through which many of the deep-sea sailors travelled, and from which many of them never returned. The statistics relating to injury were high; but there was a good deal of illness as well. One might, for example, have imagined that scurvy had long been conquered. But, even in the second half of the nineteenth century, it was still occurring alarmingly often. Indeed, in 1873, the number of cases actually began to increase, and the Board of Trade had to issue a circular on the subject. It pointed out that: "Lime juice [which had taken the place of lemon juice as a preventative] *of itself* will not prevent scurvy, and that too much reliance is placed on it to the neglect of varied food

Very gradually conditions for ships' crews improved, and better food formed an important part of this improvement. But it was not until late in the nineteenth century that ship owners had to let a sailor know the type of food on board before he signed on.

scales." And: "That lime juice, in connection with fresh or preserved meat and vegetables, may prevent scurvy.

"That dietary scale of ships should, therefore, include a fair proportion of fresh and 'preserved' meats, as distinguished from 'salted' meats."

Shipowners were warned that, though "it is not at present desirable to insert a statutory scale of diet in the Articles of Agreement with crews serving on long voyages, though it may possibly be necessary hereafter, unless shipowners themselves move in the matter."

If the shipowners were slow to move, the required legislation was equally laggardly. In 1875, there were fifty-eight outbreaks of the disease; in 1881, ninety-nine – and that was exactly three times the 1866 figure.

The Articles of Agreement were contained in a document which the sailor signed at the beginning of the voyage. It was a form of contract, binding him to the ship for a specified period, and listing his rights. Some of the men did not read it; many were unable to; and a few were either so drunk or so hung-over, that they would happily have signed away their lives. Had they studied it more carefully, they might have realized that this, precisely, was what they were doing.

Later on, the Board of Trade was forced to make good its threat, and compel owners to stipulate the scale of food to be provided. The "limits" of the voyage were supposed to be defined in the Articles; but

these could be as long as anyone cared to make them. There was also a list of misdemeanours and their penalties. From the mariner's viewpoint, it all added up to very little. In any case, few of them took the document seriously. When, in some foreign port, they found another captain looking for hands and promising better pay, they had no compunction about deserting.

As late in the century as 1889, the *Daily Telegraph* was reporting that the average seaman's menu added up to: "Warm water and peas for soup, pork of acrid taste and greenish hue . . . a black liquor full of short sticks called tea. . . ." Confronted by an attitude which cared so little for their comfort, who could blame sailors for deserting?

Above and below. Although the officers continued to have better food and accommodation than the crews, storms and rough seas upset meals for officers and men alike.

Seamen's Pay and Quality of Seamanship

Wages varied according to the route. When gold was discovered in New South Wales in 1851, some of the ship-owners hit upon an ingenious way of making savings in the bill of payment. Sailors were invited to sign on for a one-way voyage to Australia in return for £1 per month. Who cared that they were, more or less, being asked to give their services for nothing! At the far end of the voyage, there was masses of gold. With a bit of luck, they might make their fortunes.

Even in normal times, the payment for trips to Australia compared badly with voyages to America. In 1850, for instance, a sailor in an American-bound vessel received fifty shillings (£2.50) a month – against forty-five shillings (£2.25) for the passage to Australia and a mere forty shillings (£2) for the East Indies and China run. Steamships always paid better than their less affluent competitors in sail. In 1881,

Steamships needed a new type of sailor – the engineer. Without the technical skills of these men engines either broke down or were not used to their full potential.

the rate for steam on the American route was eighty shillings (£4) a month against sixty (£3) for sail. On the run to the East Indies and China, there was ten shillings (50p.) difference (sixty shillings in a sailing vessel and seventy [£3.50] for steam). At this time, the sailing ships to Australia were quoting fifty shillings a month. No figures were given for steamers. Higher wages account for the fact that there was seldom any difficulty in recruiting men for the unpleasant and arduous job of feeding coal into the furnaces of the early steamships. Plenty of sailors were only too eager to change their trade and become firemen.

The long and the short of it, then, was that sailors were being ill paid, ill nourished, and ill accommodated for very hard and dangerous work. A few owners realized this. William Inman, founder of the Inman Line, was one. In 1860, he observed: "A good wage will secure good men. . . . If men are well treated in the forecastle, and well paid, the ship-owner does not need the assistance of the State in order to enable him to obtain excellent crews." Unlike many enterprises, the company preferred to employ married men ("if they can get them").

Ideally, before a master set off on his voyage, he should have gained some idea of the kind of men he was about to command. Whenever a seaman was discharged, his previous captain was supposed to give him a reference. But, as the British Consul at Le Havre said, "It is surprising how few captains have the moral courage to refuse good characters to those who are unworthy of them; and yet the evils, and even danger, of not doing so are patent to every one."

No doubt the reason was that, after a long voyage, a master had many things to think about – and that he, no less than anyone else, was looking forward to a spell on dry land. He did not wish to waste precious moments arguing about whether a particular man was, or was not, a good seaman of trusty character. If he had referred to the relevant section of the

The arrival of the *Great Eastern* in New York, 1860. Better pay for crews on the new steamships on the American route meant that there was seldom a shortage of recruits for their crews.

Merchant Shipping Act of 1854, however, he would have found that he was liable to be punished for giving a "false character" to a discharged member of his crew.

British consuls, on the whole, seem invariably to have taken an unenthusiastic view of their country's mariners. For example, the representative in the Azores, when asked for his opinion, said: "I do not see any particular feature to note in the general condition of seamen in my port except their habitual tendency to intoxication." He probably had dark memories of extracting men from the local gaol.

Sailors came in two classes; Able Seamen and Ordinary Seamen. The former were men of skill and experience, and any master who left port without enough of them on board did so at his peril. The question was: how to differentiate between the two. Could a certificate of competency be issued? A commission was appointed to consider the idea, but it presently came to the conclusion that such a move would be both unpopular and impossible. "The proposal to give [such a certificate]," it reported, "was very carefully considered by the members . . . and they could not see how it could be done. They could not make the government responsible for his competency, and for the fact of his previous service; and they thought that any attempt to do so would be illusory."

A few years later, in 1871, a committee representing the Liverpool shipowners, took a less negative view. Accepting the need for some proof of a man's ability, they noted that "Men often obtain AB rating after one or two voyages, though they are incompetent to perform the most ordinary duties of a sailor. Many masters state that out of crews of twenty and twenty-five, not more than three or four know the compass, can steer, heave the lead, or perform any other of the duties of the seaman."

The members suggested that an able seaman should receive a higher rate of pay than his less knowledgeable colleague. This would give him

Overleaf. A boarding party prepares for action with cutlasses and muskets.

The crew of the Royal Navy's training ship H.M.S. *Excellent* queue for their morning beer in the ship's canteen, 1881.

an incentive to study and to sit the necessary examination. The test would be short, simple, and practical. He would, however, be required to produce evidence of having served for a specified period at sea. In the case of lads who had been apprenticed in government training ships, only two years would be necessary. For others, four years would be needed. Later, the committee revised its idea, and decided that the examination could be dispensed with. Only the period of service at sea would be required.

According to some startling figures produced by that untiring student of maritime affairs, the British Consul in the Azores, many of the masters of smaller vessels could, themselves, do with some tutoring in their art. In a table published in 1843, he noted that, in vessels ranging from 41 to 60 tons, 53 captains were "of sober habits, but not acquainted with the mode of ascertaining longitude." As for shipmasters commanding vessels of 61 to 80 tons, 11 of them were "of intemperate habits, and not acquain-

Training naval crews: recruits receiving torpedo instruction on H.M.S. *Excellent*, 1881.

Gun drill on a man of war in 1873, before the coming of turrets to house the ship's guns.

ted with the mode of ascertaining longitude." It all added up to the need for officers' certificates. As already noted in the previous chapter, these came about in 1850. During the seven intervening years, heaven knows how many ships were lost in the fruit trade between Britain and the Azores – simply because their masters were lost or drunk or both.

The Scandal of the Ports

Of all the characters in the nineteenth century, the sailor was probably the most innocent – or, at least, the most out of touch. He was encased in his vessel for months at a time: a citizen of a minute community, who rarely came face-to-face with the rest of the world. Before the introduction of wireless telegraphy, his only source of information was another ship. War might have broken out; London might have been set ablaze; his family might have been murdered; and he would have known nothing about it. Much of his working life was occupied by the twin problems of receiving enough to eat and getting enough sleep. Both of these elemental needs were in short supply.

At sea, a man did what he was told. Unless he was an officer, the need to make decisions was minimal. Such a life-style made him no match for the wiles of people on shore. This shortcoming might have been less distressing had there not been, in every port of the world, a considerable number of characters who awaited his arrival with eagerness. These were the crimps and the runners, the brothel-keepers and the publicans, the con-men and the thieves, who saw, in this naive and much-exploited sailor a source of easy money. The lives of these scoundrels were made a great deal easier by the masters of vessels likely to be in port for some time (it could be weeks or, even, months) discharging cargo and awaiting a fresh load. There was little work for the men to do on these occasions: certainly not sufficient to justify the expenses of food and wages. If this unsavoury mob spirited them away, the bill in terms of manpower would add up to a lot less.

The human content of this package was villainous enough; but an even greater peril – from which almost everything else stemmed – was an apparently innocent piece of paper known as an "advance note." The idea behind it was harmless. It promised the sailor an advance of at least one month's (probably two) pay – to enable him to repay his debts on shore, and to kit himself out for the coming trip.

No one could argue about the need for a seaman to buy adequate clothing. Sir Thomas Brassey refers to an owner whose "captains had often told him that, in bad weather, they had given their own clothes to the man at the wheel, to enable him to remain at his post." And the President of the Bristol Chamber of Commerce "had frequently seen them going on board ships belonging to his firm in such a destitute condition that the police would have been justified in apprehending them for passing through the streets insufficiently clad." In this respect, the merchant service could well have learned a lesson from the Royal Navy, where every ship had a supply of clothing on board in what was called the "slop chest." But: no. Instead, these ridiculous pieces of paper were provided. In a well-ordered world, they might have worked. As things were, they were seldom used for the purposes intended.

For as long as the sailor kept his advance note, the owners would not redeem it until he was on board ship and safely at sea again. Members of the port fraternity of scoundrels, on the other hand, would be happy to advance him the cash. Since he probably had a massive thirst, and his enforced abstinence had sharpened his appetite for women, there was no problem about how to spend it.

What happened was this. A tailor would offer to fit the man out. At some point, the crimp would come into the picture, and suggest a night on the town: plenty of drink, girls, all that sort of thing. After that, if the by-now-very-jolly jack tar drank himself unconscious, there would be little else to do. If he had a strong head, and making him paralytic looked like becoming expensive, a drop of dope (laudanum was a popular variety) would speed things up. The sleeping sailor was then dumped on board his ship, and the master was presented with the advance note and a bill for clothing. He settled the account, and the sailor was faced with the prospect of working for one or two months with no reward (the period was referred to as "dead horse") – to repay a loan on which the interest had been unpardonably high. The situation is well

The dock area of a big city was an unpleasant place. The inhabitants, mostly pimps, prostitutes and con men, set out to rob sailors. In this they were usually all too successful.

summed up in a shanty entitled *The Liverpool Judies*:

> "The next I remembers I woke in the morn.
> On a three skys'l yarder bound south round Cape Horn;
> Wid an ol' suit of oilskins, and two pair o' sox,
> An' a bloomin' big 'ead, and a sea-chest of rocks."

This was the operation at its more simple. Shanghaing* took a little bit longer. The seaman was lured by "runners" to a boarding house. Girls, mostly recruited from a local brothel, would be in attendance. He would be promised a good time: comfortable accommodation and plenty of good food. The process of rendering him unconscious would then begin. Once he was "out for the count," his advance note would be cashed. He might end up in the same vessel as that in which he had arrived. He might, equally well, find himself on board some hulk, bound for a port at which it was difficult to find a return passage. The rate for this human merchandise varied from port to port. In San Francisco, the crimp was paid five dollars a head. Cases have even been recorded of dead men soused in rum – sold as "drunken sailors" to officers who didn't examine their purchases too carefully.

Nobody, unless he was on guard, was safe. There was even the case of a mate who went ashore for an evening's pleasure in Newcastle, New South Wales. When he woke up in the morning, he had a sore head, and found that he had been shanghaied back on board his own ship as a deck hand!

Herman Melville described "the variety of land-sharks, land-rats, and other vermin which make the helpless mariner their prey. In the shape of landlords, clothiers, barkeepers, crimps and boarding house loungers,

By the end of the nineteenth century the Royal Navy was setting an example with better conditions for sailors, although the merchant service was slow to follow. This is the accommodation of the hospital ship H.M.S. *Melbourne*.

* The name was derived from that of the Chinese port, Shanghai – from which it was particularly difficult to find a berth on a homeward bound ship.

A steward, serving in the first-class dining area of an Atlantic steamship, tries to stay upright during rough weather.

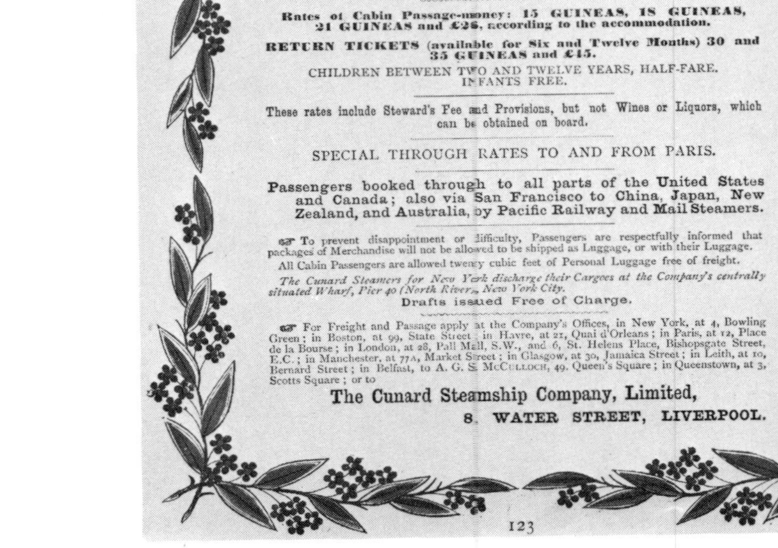

CUNARD LINE.

ROYAL MAIL STEAMERS.

ALEPPO.	CATALONIA.	MALTA.	PAVONIA.	SERVIA.
AURANIA.	CEPHALONIA	MARATHON.	SAMARIA.	SIDON.
ATLAS.	DEMERARA.	MOROCCO.	SARAGOSSA.	TARIFA.
BATAVIA.	GALLIA.	PALMYRA.	SCYTHIA.	TRINIDAD.
BOTHNIA.	KEDAR.	PARTHIA.		

From Liverpool every Saturday for New York, and every Wednesday for Boston, calling at Queenstown the following day.

From New York every Wednesday, and from Boston every Saturday for Queenstown and Liverpool.

NOTICE.—With the view of diminishing the chances of Collision, the Steamers of this Line take a specified course for all seasons of the year.

On the Outward Passage from Queenstown to New York or Boston, crossing Meridian of 50 at 43 Lat., or nothing to the North of 43. On the Homeward Passage, crossing the Meridian 50 at 42 Lat., or nothing to the North of 42.

Rates of Cabin Passage-money: 15 GUINEAS, 18 GUINEAS, 21 GUINEAS and £26, according to the accommodation.

RETURN TICKETS (available for Six and Twelve Months) 30 and 35 GUINEAS and £45.

CHILDREN BETWEEN TWO AND TWELVE YEARS, HALF-FARE. INFANTS FREE.

These rates include Steward's Fee and Provisions, but not Wines or Liquors, which can be obtained on board.

SPECIAL THROUGH RATES TO AND FROM PARIS.

Passengers booked through to all parts of the United States and Canada; also via San Francisco to China, Japan, New Zealand, and Australia, by Pacific Railway and Mail Steamers.

☞ To prevent disappointment or difficulty, Passengers are respectfully informed that packages of Merchandise will not be allowed to be shipped as Luggage, or with their Luggage.

All Cabin Passengers are allowed twenty cubic feet of Personal Luggage free of freight.

The Cunard Steamers for New York discharge their Cargoes at the Company's centrally situated Wharf, Pier 40 (North River), New York City.

Drafts issued Free of Charge.

☞ For Freight and Passage apply at the Company's Offices, in New York, at 4, Bowling Green; in Boston, at 99, State Street; in Havre, at 21, Quai d'Orleans; in Paris, at 12, Place de la Bourse; in London, at 28, Pall Mall, S.W., and 6, St. Helens Place, Bishopsgate Street, E.C.; in Manchester, at 77A, Market Street; in Glasgow, at 30, Jamaica Street; in Leith, at 10, Bernard Street; in Belfast, to A. G. S. McCulloch, 49, Queen's Square; in Queenstown, at 3, Scotts Square; or to

The Cunard Steamship Company, Limited,
8, WATER STREET, LIVERPOOL.

123

A publicity leaflet issued by the Cunard Steamship Company in 1883.

the land-sharks devour him limb by limb; while the land-rats and mice constantly nibble at his purse."

In a report prepared by a Dr. Smith entitled *The Sailor and the Service at the Port of New York*, the author had the following to say: "But let us suppose the sailor returns with the runner to his old boarding-house. What kind of place is prepared for his reception? Few that have not had actual experience would credit a faithful description of the vile dens. Situated in the very worst parts of the city . . . in old dilapidated houses, reeking with filth and overrun with vermin, the sailor is shown to a bunk in a room that has as many double, and in some cases treble, tiers as it will hold, and without a sign of a convenience for the ordinary necessities of life; and that is his lodging place. In the saloon, or living room of the house, he is surrounded by a crowd of creatures, male and female, in various stages of intoxication; and can it be thought strange if, under such circumstances, he immediately proceeds to get as drunk as his associates? How can he escape? Each newcomer is expected to contribute to the hilarity of the crowd, and he would be forthwith thrashed and then pitched into the street if he failed to meet such expectations."

Every big seaport had its equivalent. In Hamburg there was Saint Pauli (now eagerly visited by tourists who hope to witness vice from the safety of plush seats), Calcutta had Flag Street, Yokohama had the Kuruwa, and London was certainly not immune. Incoming vessels on the Thames were invaded by crimps and runners to such an extent that police protection had to be provided. During the first six months of 1868, out of 406 ships examined by Board of Trade officials, crimps were found aboard 130. For the corresponding period of 1874, out of 503, the "port-sharks" were only on board 4.

But perhaps the most effective blow to this unsavoury traffic occurred on 1st August, 1881, when advance notes were abolished.

Improvement in Conditions

The prospect for the sailor was beginning to look brighter. In 1889, the National Union of Seamen (then called the National Amalgamated Sailors' and Firemen's Union of Great Britain and Northern Ireland) was able to report a membership of 65,000 and branches in nearly every port. Its aims were:

"1. To make allowances to members on the security of their wages and allotment notes.
2. To establish reasonable hours of duty, and a fair rate of pay.
3. To secure improved conditions aboard ship.
4. To establish proper homes for seamen in the ports.
5. To obtain compensation for accidents, and provide legal help.
6. To establish claims for compensation with respect to salvage and loss of wages; also to protect members in other ways from undesirable people such as crimps and other pests in port."

Even the *Daily Telegraph*, not normally given to enthusing over a manifestation of labour's solidarity, found reason to applaud. "There is nothing that is not laudable and praiseworthy in this scheme," observed an editorial writer.

As the nineteenth century gave way to the twentieth, conditions on board ship became appreciably better. When the White Star liner *Olympic* came into service in 1911, Dr. W. E. Home recorded, "the sailors and the engine-room staff live forward in cabins, very like those of third-class passengers, but not all the beds are up to that quality, for there were several of the 'donkey's breakfast' pattern – beds stuffed with straw. Their cabins (each has in it a washing basin) generally berth three men; the three will rarely be there together." The *Achilles* of the Blue Funnel Line had a deck house situated at the after end, in which her European crew members were berthed, and a library "from which her crew can get books." The ABs had two-berth cabins, each with a port hole, and opening into a mess room with a sky light. A freight-liner (anonymous) inspected by Dr. Home received less favourable comment. However, the forecastle accommodation did, at least, have a lavatory – and that was a considerable improvement on most of her predecessors.

The captain of a merchant ship posing on his ship's rail in 1896.

7 *War and Peace*

Without war, or the immediate threat of it, the armed forces make little progress. Towards the latter end of the nineteenth century, there were many critics who professed that, if one discounted the introduction of the steam engine, the Royal Navy had hardly changed since Nelson's day. But, as its defenders might have pointed out, there had been no need. The only major war had been the Crimean (1854–55), which had taken place a great many miles away from United Kingdom waters, and which had not been noted for its naval engagements. At no time had the security of Britain's coastline been threatened: indeed, during most of Queen Victoria's reign, the crews of men-of-war seldom had to do more than practice manoeuvres and gunnery, and to look nice on the occasions when the Queen reviewed her ships. Even "gunboat diplomacy" had done little to tax the Admiralty's resources. As its name suggested, all that was needed was a gunboat – and not a very big one, at that.

There had, of course, been the abolition of flogging (though not formally). Many officers watched its departure with regret; and none more so than the author of a book entitled *The Midshipman's Friend.* Writing in 1845, he asked his young readers to believe that there was nothing beastly about it. The unpleasant ceremony was carried out "with a solemnity and feeling truly impressive." No doubt the victim's feelings were even more impressive. If it were to go, there would still have to be "some *extreme* punishment:" possibly something worse, a torture that would "make even a cannibal blush for his country."

Only retired naval officers, who had found that its rewards made a pleasant addition to their pensions, viewed the departure of impressment with any regret. Pressed men were not popular with the majority of commanders, who preferred their ships to be manned by volunteers. The latter obviously went about their duties with greater enthusiasm than sullen characters, who had been driven into the Navy against their will.

The press gang method would never return. Nevertheless, there had to be some means of increasing the Navy's manpower in times of war. Denuding a homeward-bound merchantman of her crew, or taking sailors off the streets in seaports, had one considerable advantage. The men might not be able to fire guns, or to drill, or to conduct themselves in a manner becoming to a member of the Royal Navy; but at least they knew how to handle sails, and how to carry out the other tasks necessary

Opposite. One of the first submarines passing H.M.S. *Victory* at Portsmouth in 1902.

to drive a ship. They had only to learn how to fight, and they were ready for active service.

Part-time Sailors

In an attempt to fulfil this need, the Royal Naval Reserve was created in 1859. Designed to make part-time Naval personnel out of merchant seamen, the original strength, as laid down by the Manning Commission of that year, specified 60,000 officers and men – of which, 10,000 would be responsible for the defence of the coastline, and would not be required to travel more than 150 miles from U.K. shores. Among the critics of the new scheme was the MP for Hastings, Thomas Brassey (later Earl Brassey). "The Naval Reserve," he wrote in 1877, "was established with the view of putting an end to panics, of frequent occurrence, and reflecting little credit on the nation. No attempt, however, has yet been made to establish the thorough system of training which constituted the pith and marrow of the scheme of the Manning Commission of 1859."

Brassey was not the only one to have doubts about the idea. The response of merchant seamen was disappointing. The shipping master of Poplar, deep in the Port of London, expressed the opinion that "only a small proportion of seamen join the Reserve, because of the difficulty experienced in making up the necessary time for the drills between the date of a ship's arrival and her departure on a fresh voyage." The sailors' wives were also against the scheme – largely, it appears, because they were under "erroneous impressions as to the duties involved, and the liability of the men to be called upon to serve in the Navy." (Brassey.)

The older Naval officers thought little of the notion – not because they doubted the seamanship of the reservists, but because they were uncertain whether merchant service officers would be able to adapt themselves to the traditions and style of the Royal Navy. Not that they were offering them very much: from the start, it was made clear that, in wartime, a reservist officer could expect little likelihood of receiving a command. Even experienced shipmasters had to be content with the rank of Sub-Lieutenant, which was only a degree or two higher than a Midshipman (in the larger warships, Sub-Lieutenants inhabited the gun room, which was the midshipmen's mess. Only Lieutenants and above were allowed into the ward room).

But then, it must be admitted, the older Naval officers of this period were very old indeed. When somebody expressed anxiety about this incipient senility, somebody else pointed out that, about one hundred years previously, Admiral Sir John Norris had served with sufficient distinction in the War of Jenkins's Ear. Sir John had been eighty-four at the time.

Admiral of the Fleet, Lord Fisher of Kilverstone: the architect of the Royal Navy as it was at the outbreak of the First World War.

The Changing Navy

In 1841, an event had occurred which, although the Navy was completely unaware of it, was to have the most profound effect on the future of the service. This was the birth of John Arbuthnot Fisher. "Jackie" Fisher entered the Navy in 1854. When he witnessed his first flogging, he fainted – which may have been to his discredit. He was often sick at sea, which was not regarded with disfavour. After all, Nelson himself had

The Royal Navy had been slow to recognize the skill and status of ship's engineers. By 1895, when this photograph was taken, they had at last been awarded Royal Commissions.

frequently been unwell in bad weather. But these were details: the important thing about Fisher, as soon became clear, was the new outlook he brought to the service.

He possessed incredible energy, a genius for organization, a mind which thrived on innovations, and a realistic approach to the art of warfare. He believed that it was: "... the essence of violence;" that moderation in War is imbecility; "that one must 'HIT FIRST. HIT HARD. KEEP ON HITTING.'"

As his power increased, his attitude to the ageing warships of the Fleet was summed up in a note to the First Lord, the Earl of Selborne. "Scrap the lot," he advised. In his attitude to vessels, as to everything and everyone else, Fisher was ruthless. But it paid. The completion, in 1906, of HMS *Dreadnought*, which was Fisher-inspired, set a new standard for battleships throughout the world. Battle cruisers (faster ships, heavily armed but more lightly armoured) were introduced by him two years later. They were less successful (the armour was too thin), but they, too, were revolutionary. The old officers, with whom the Navy had been burdened for too long, would never have sanctioned them.

H.M.S. *Dreadnought*, the battleship which, when she came into service in 1906, made everything else seem obsolete.

Fisher was concerned with ships and their deployment. The Navy which went to war in August, 1914, was largely of his designing, and the men who comprised it adored him. Admittedly, he made many enemies among his peers (notably Admiral Lord Charles Beresford), but junior officers thought the world of him – not least, because he actually encouraged them to express new ideas. Before his arrival at the top, this would have been unheard of.

As a reformer of conditions on the lower deck, his influence was less marked – largely because there had already been so many improvements. The sailors were treated more humanely; and, according to a publication entitled *With The Fleet* describing "Life in a Cruiser," which was put out in 1905, the now completely accepted steam engine had even succeeded in removing the peril from storms at sea. "Scarcely have the active seamen time to make their arrangements," the author wrote, "before *the gale is upon us*. It could be wished that we had more sea room, but there are frowning rocks, now white-capped by the force of the blast, and doubtless dangers only known to the experienced navigator. Hark! What is that startling cry as we seem to swerve towards the nearest coast, and the rush of men in ordered disorder along the gangways? Be not appalled! those in charge of the vessel are equal to the emergency. It is the steam steering gear that has failed us at this critical moment, but the seamen

A petty officers' room at a newly-opened naval shore barracks at Portsmouth.

Although efforts were made to improve the conditions of life in the Royal Navy, the Admiralty was powerless against the weather and the sea. H.M.S. *Terrible* battles through rough seas in 1902.

have already got the ship under control, the hand wheel which so well served the *Discovery* in her Antarctic exploration is smartly manipulated by the strenuous sailor, and the ship once more steadied on her course.

"Thanks to our powerful engines, we have no difficulty in passing through the vortex of the storm, and soon bright gleams of sunshine ahead point to a recurrence of finer weather to grace the termination of our pleasant cruise."

When the ship arrived in port, "The merry crew are permitted to assemble on the quarter-deck where they entertain themselves and their friends, the visitors, with songs, shanties, and horn-pipes." The publication was issued as a souvenir for the Naval Exhibition, which took place that year. Consequently, its enthusiasm is understandable – if suspect. The author was doubtless aware of the plight of numerous sailing ships which, at the mercy of the wind's direction, had been driven ashore by gales. Nevertheless, as he failed to point out, steam presented sailors with a new kind of hazard in the form of greater speed.

All that Fisher asked of his men was that they should perform their duties better than they had ever done before. Again, he was ready to be ruthless, but there was little need for it. The ratings responded eagerly to his challenge.

Fisher's triumph in producing a Navy which fully exploited the technical resources of his day produced a new type of reservist. A talent for

On board one of Britain's first submarines in 1902. The legs belong to the Captain who is steering, the man with raised hands works the horizontal rudder that regulates depth and on the deck are the torpedoes with air cylinders above them.

handling sails and hauling on lines was no longer necessary. The vessels were steamers, pure and simple: the age had long vanished when it was thought advisable to equip a ship with sail to save coal (or to insure against a breakdown in her engines). Consequently, new skills were needed, and there seemed to be no reason why a man who was, for example, a mechanic in peacetime, should not perform a useful role at sea in wartime. Thus, in 1903, another type of reservist was introduced: the Royal Naval Volunteer Reserve. Although many of its members were amateur yachtsmen, seafaring experience was not essential (merchant seamen continued to belong to the Royal Naval Reserve).

Unfortunately, as in the case of the Royal Naval Reserve, there was a tendency to regard the newcomers as second class citizens. It was possible to single them out by their uniforms; the officers' ranks were shown by quarter-inch waved braid (as against half-inch straight for the regulars), and the three narrow white tapes on the ratings' collars were also in a wavey pattern. They branded a man as an amateur in a world which prided itself on its professionalism. Nevertheless, these all too evident marks of an inferior cast did little to deter recruits.

When, many years previously, Queen Victoria had been asked to review the requirements of a sailor's face in the Royal Navy, she decided that beards were in order, and that it was equally proper to be clean-shaven. However, in spite of her dearest Albert's moustache, she ordained that, whilst a be-whiskered upper lip might be all right for the Army (indeed, such growth might even be encouraged), it was not suitable for seafaring.

Since, in civilian life, moustaches – and big ones, at that – were in fashion, joining the R.N.V.R. required at least one sacrifice. The first

Armed naval ratings at Liverpool docks to protect shipping during the dock strike in August, 1911.

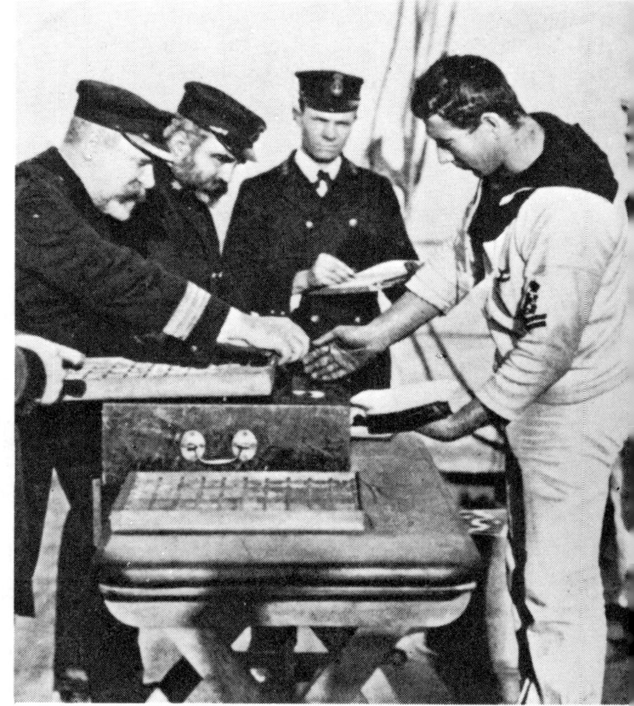

Pay day on board, *c.* 1910. After deductions the paymaster counted out the balance and the seaman swept it into his cap.

A time-honoured ritual on board ship in 1910: the effects of a dead sailor are auctioned among the crew to provide money for his widow.

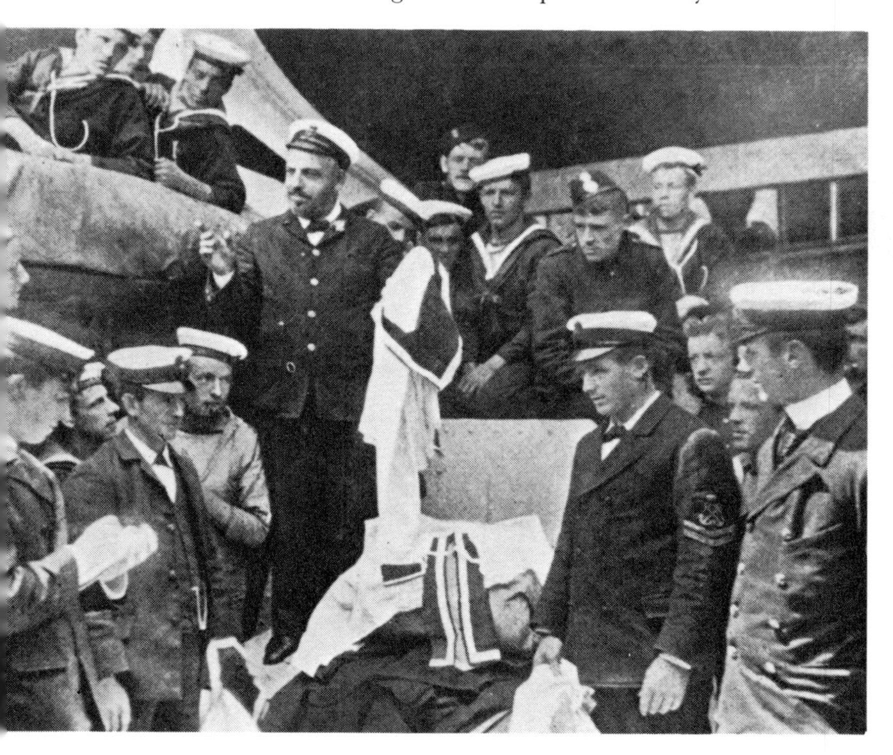

Naval ratings on board H.M.S. *Bellepheron* in 1913. The straw hats, which were only worn in summer, were soon to become outmoded.

evidence that people were willing to make it, came from the Stock Exchange, when a sizeable number of its employees marched off to a local barber's. "They returned," the *Financial Times* observed, "with that clean-shaven visage that marks the boys of the bull-dog breed. The change wrought in their facial expressions was not in every case the kind desired. Several looked very much like the typical Irish comedian, whilst others are strangely reminiscent of Dartmoor. Needless to say, the affair gave huge delight . . . and the new-created tars were made to dance a hornpipe. . . ."

The *Daily Mail* reported the Stock Exchange's eagerness to serve the country at sea by suggesting a new language for its dealings. A conversation would go like this: "Is the skipper on deck, mate?"

"Belay there with that telegram."

And: "Rands [South African currency] are a trifle choppy this morning."

The First World War

Alas – when war did break out, the dreams of many of these ardent young men were swiftly destroyed. Instead of carrying out what they considered to be the natural role of a sailor, even an amateur tar, they were organized in much the manner of infantry, and they did most of their fighting on dry land. A great many were drafted into the Naval Brigade, which attempted to deny Antwerp to the Germans in 1914. When the Belgian town fell,

The destruction of British naval and merchant shipping in both world wars cost the lives of many seamen. German U-boats in Harwich harbour after their surrender in 1918.

the score to the enemy was 7 R.N.V.R. officers and 53 men killed; 5 officers and 931 men taken prisoner. As a considerable bonus, however, 37 officers and 1,442 men sought sanctuary in Holland – where they were interned for the rest of the war in a camp at Groningen, which they christened HMS *Timber Town.*

Officers in the Royal Naval Reserve fared better, and many commanded such ships as trawlers and mine-sweepers. They brought their own peculiar nautical traditions with them. In *Swept Channels*, Taffrail recalled two vessels commanded by Reserve officers competing for position at the harbour mouth. The more senior signalled "Obey orders. Kindly don't argue." To which the other replied. "Don't you argue with me. Do you think the Cunard takes orders from a Burns Line tramp?"

On 4th August, 1914, a strike of merchant seamen was in progress at North Shields. According to the official history of the National Union of Seamen, "The Union leadership had no doubt as to what their attitude at this moment of crisis must be. Tupper, the Union organiser, was at North Shields, leading the strike, when war was declared. He did not hesitate. He called a meeting of his members and told them that the strike must be called off. To this the strikers unanimously agreed. It was a significant gesture. It meant for one thing that the Union had no intention of taking advantage of the crisis to hold the industry – and in fact the nation – up to ransom. And it demonstrated the spirit in which the seafarers of the country were to meet the multiplied perils to which the ships of the Merchant Navy would inevitably be exposed."

To the normal hazards of the sea were now added those of the surface raider and the U-boat. It was not until the latter developed its technique of underwater warfare, that the casualties became alarming. Indeed, the surface raiders – as personified by SNS *Emden* – were very gentlemanly in their transactions. Before a merchant vessel was sunk, her crew was taken off – and, eventually, conveyed to safety. There was even one case in which the German cruiser sent her boat back to a ship about to be destroyed – to rescue a seaman's motorcycle, which happened to be on board.

U-boats were another matter. As this menace became more pronounced, the Admiralty agreed that, when a ship under charter was sunk, her crew should be given the fare to their home ports – plus pay of up to fifteen days until they reached home. When the ship-owners were asked to follow this very praiseworthy example, most of them refused.

So far as naval occasions on the surface were concerned, the only battle of any magnitude fought by the Navy was Jutland – which, by its very indecisiveness, provided a source for argument which, even now, shows few signs of running dry. For an impression of what it felt like to fire and be fired upon during this period, a better source is a journal kept by an officer who was present at the sinking of the German cruiser *Koenigsberg* in the Rufiji River (East Africa) on a July day in 1915. Act One finds the German vessel firing its guns at the British force. Thus: "We heard the boom; then, before it had finished, came Whizz-z-z-z or plop, plop, plop, plop, as the shells went just short or over. They were firing much more rapidly than we, and I should think more accurately, but if I had been in the *Koenigsberg*, I should, probably, have thought the opposite."

After a while, however, the superiority of the British force began to tell. "In a very short time," the officer wrote, "there was a big explosion from the direction of the *Koenigsberg*, and from then on she was never free from smoke – sometimes more, sometimes less; one moment belching out clouds of black smoke, then yellow with dull explosions from time to time. We kept on firing regularly ourselves, one salvo to the minute – or, perhaps, two salvoes in three minutes, but the gun-layers were told to keep cool and make sure of their aim. There was one enormous explosion which shot up twice as high as the *Koenigsberg*'s masts, and the resulting smoke was visible from our deck. The men sent up a huge cheer."

The responsibilities of the men on the lower deck were to do what they were told. The tools of their trade might have changed, but that was all. For the officers, however, the First World War brought a new challenge. As a contemporary naval observer (Arthur Hungerford Pollen) pointed out, "If steam has done much to lessen the perils of the sea, speed, the product of steam, has added to them."

Wrote Mr. Pollen: "The sailor . . . even in times of peace, passes his days, and still more his nights, encompassed by the threat of irreparable disaster. An oversight that may take thirty seconds to commit – and a hundred deaths, a wrecked ship, and a shattered reputation [are the] reward for thirty years of constant and unblemished devotion to duty."

As became rapidly clear, the war which had promised "a land fit for heroes to live in," achieved nothing of the kind. Nor were things very much better at sea. The Royal Navy was compelled to abide by the Washington Treaty, which stipulated that no nation should build any battleships for the next ten years. After that, additions to the Fleet should conform to a maximum tonnage (35,000). The result was that they were considerably inferior to the juggernauts planned by Hitler, who had no time for such treaties – and, in any case, had not been a signatory to the Washington document. (It is, perhaps, salutory to recall that it required 3 battleships, 2 battle cruisers, 2 aircraft carriers, 4 cruisers, and sundry destroyers to track down the *Bismarck* and destroy her.)

Children's deck games on board one of the great ocean liners.

Atlantic Liners

There were, however, no restrictions on the size of those other maritime giants – the Atlantic liners. Now, regrettably, killed by the introduction of jet airliners, they were not only very fine ships: they were, to all intents and purposes, very luxurious floating hotels. The first half of the twentieth century was the golden age of this type of ship: *Mauretania*, *Olympic*, *Aquitania*, *Berengaria*, and so on, each a very model of sumptuous accommodation, wonderful food and excellent service. The stewards who ministered to the passengers brought the skills of the Ritz and the Savoy to the ocean route. They were attentive and highly observant. They no doubt enjoyed their work; but, as everyone else, they did it for money. A considerable portion of their incomes came from tips.

In *The North Atlantic Run*, John Maxtone-Graham, a veteran of many Atlantic crossings, has this to say: "In the late thirties, cabin and dining-room stewards were tipped five dollars [about £2] and a bath steward two. If these sums seem insignificant for a crossing's work, it is worth remembering that dollars were more substantial in those days. Deck

The Cunard liner *Queen Mary*, one of the great floating hotel ships of the era between the two world wars.

stewards made smaller tips but had many more clients. The men in the smoking room made drink tips in addition to their cut from the [swimming] pools.

"Intelligence about a tipper, good or bad, spread as though by bush telegraph. Once branded by the first to be tipped, the passenger's reputation for extravagance or avarice preceded him from cabin to dining room to deck chair to smoking room and on to the pier. A bad tipper invariably advertised himself the first day out by announcing in a hectoring tone: 'You take care of me, steward, and I'll take care of you.' Among the worst tippers were film stars, who had a habit of passing out eight-by-ten glossies of themselves eastbound and compounding the insult by autographing them westbound."

But, writes Mr. Maxtone-Graham, "If I have dwelt on stewards and their tips, it has not been my intention to characterize them as grasping opportunists whose zeal was governed by passenger exorbitance. They were, in fact, loyal company servants whose cheerful competence was one of the enormous attractions of ocean travel."

The Great Depression

This was the happier side of sea travel. For the British seamen's union on shore, there were problems. In 1926, Britain was paralysed by the General Strike – and the union's officials caused considerable controversy by refusing to take part in it. It was the only member of the Trades' Union Congress to abstain. "Their main contention," says the Union's history, "was that they could not take action without the consent, obtained by ballot vote, of their membership, nor could they justify the breaking of their agreements with the shipowners." This decision, not unnaturally, angered the T.U.C., and things were made even worse when the seamen's president, Havelock Wilson, decided to support a break-away, non-political, organization named the Miners' Industrial Union. In a moment of pique, the 1928 Congress decided, unanimously, to expel the seamen. By the following year, however, all was forgiven. The National Union of Seamen withdrew its association with the Miners' Industrial Union, and the T.U.C. welcomed it fondly back into the fold.

But, by then, the depression in world trade had caused the lot of the British merchant seaman to become very bad indeed.

The slump swept across the Atlantic from the United States with all the power of a storm force wind. By 1932, there were 40,000 seamen unemployed, and 1,663,000 tons of British shipping laid up (the figure for the earlier years of the depression had been 368,000). Freight rates dropped from one all-time low to another; and the situation was not helped by owners who sold off their vessels cheaply to foreign firms – who then sailed them back into British ports, offering to carry freight at little more than peppercorn rates. As the general secretary of the N.U.S. announced: "In our ports lie hundreds of ships, practically derelict, not through age or unseaworthiness, but because parliaments and governments and the anonymous financial dictatorships behind them are pursuing policies which aim deliberately at the restriction of international trade."

These were, no doubt, harsh words. But the seamen in jobs were facing

The sinking of H.M.S. *Ark Royal*, December 1941. Despite the emergency, the survivors, in disciplined formation on the flight deck, wait to be rescued.

the prospects of a wage cut; the majority were, as the saying goes, "rotting on the beach;" and, to add to it all, many of the men were given the galling sight of produce from the British Empire being brought into British ports by foreign steamers.

In 1935, thankfully, the health of British industry began to perk up. Two years later, the owners were beginning to place orders for new tonnage. So far as the designs of these vessels were concerned, a new rule had come into force. The plans for the crew's quarters had to be submitted to the Board of Trade for approval: and, what was more, they could not be up front in the forecastle, or below the load water-line, except in very small vessels. There had to be adequate lighting and heating and ventilation: enough space for recreation, hospital accommodation, and proper mess rooms. The days of the hell-ships were over. From now onwards, things could only go from better to really good.

The Second World War

Or: that was how it may have seemed. Unfortunately, there was a rude interruption to progress by World War II. Britain's first major casualty was a merchant ship; the Cunarder *Athenia*, which was torpedoed by the U30 on the day war broke out. The U-boat's captain was acting in defiance of orders from Hitler; and, after the war, it was discovered that the relevant pages had been torn out of the log. But, as a demonstration of what the war held in store for merchant seamen, nothing could have been more convincing.

A happier example of a German officer's attitude to merchant shipping is provided by Captain Langsdorf of the *Graf Spee*. Before scuttling his vessel off Montevideo, Langsdorf had sunk nine British merchant ships totalling 50,000 tons – and yet he never caused a single casualty. The victims were put on board the raider's supply ship, *Altmark*, which was finally cornered in a Norwegian fjord by the destroyer *Cossack*. When the *Altmark* was boarded, she was found to have 299 prisoners on board.

The Navy always looked after her own. Commercial enterprises could not necessarily be relied on to do likewise. Nevertheless, torpedoed

January 1942: the four survivors of a merchant ship torpedoed by the Germans during the battle of the Atlantic are finally rescued by the crew of a British battleship.

Dinner time on the cramped mess deck of a British armed merchant cruiser during the Second World War.

merchant seamen were treated tolerably well during the Second World War. They received full pay until returning to the U.K., or being offered another job. Back in Britain, each was entitled to fourteen days special shipwreck leave on full pay – plus any normal leave that had accumulated.

They thoroughly deserved it. This is one man's account (recalled in a conversation with the author) of what happened to him shortly after the battleship *Barham* was sunk by four torpedoes fired by a U-boat: "The list was getting worse than ever, and it was happening quickly. Now the handrail was up in the air, and it was impossible to walk along the deck. I went in the direction of the rail, which was rather like walking up the side of a mountain.

"By now, *Barham* was lying on her side. I slid down on to one of the anti-torpedo 'blisters;' and then, as the ship lurched over at an even steeper angle, I made my way towards the bilge. Part of the ship's bottom was now clear of the water.

"Then one of the magazines blew up. The blast from it pitched me into the sea. At the same time, *Barham* began to sink. For what seemed like ages, I felt myself being sucked downwards. There was another explosion – it sounded as if it came from under water, and the force of it seemed to push me away from the ship.

"After a long interval (or that's what it seemed like), I came to the surface. Fuel oil had got into my eyes and, for some time, I floundered around without being able to see. Then my vision cleared, and the sight of a lifebelt floating on the surface a few yards away reminded me of my predicament. I had come away without one. I swam towards it: grasped hold of it, and began to blow it up. But then I found it hadn't got a stopper. I had to plug the valve with one of my fingers. I swam on until I was able to catch hold of a short piece of timber.

"Then I spotted a carley float, and there was just enough room for me on it. I stayed on board it with the other chap until, not long afterwards, a destroyer picked us up."

H.M.S. *Hood*: the last of the big battle cruisers. An epoch in naval strategy went up in smoke when the *Bismarck* sank her in 1941. Only three men of a crew totalling 1,419 survived.

During World War II, the Royal Navy lost 50,758 men killed, 820 missing, and 14,663 wounded. The Merchant Navy lost 30,248 men through enemy action.

A New Deal for Sailors

In peace, the improvement in conditions afloat, which had begun in the years immediately before the war, continued. In 1960, the men in the Merchant Navy were granted a 5½-day week (a forty-four hour week in port) and a 7½ per cent. pay rise. Thus, an AB previously receiving £33.25 a month now got £35.75. Among the media which applauded it was *The Times*, which described it as "a good agreement by any standards." As for the National Union of Seamen, they hailed it as "one of the biggest steps forward we have ever been able to secure in a single set of negotiations."

Phrases such as "the public rooms are all air-conditioned," ". . . accommodation is situated on the upper decks: most of the cabins are single-berth," and "decorated in restful colours," might seem to refer to passenger accommodation. In fact, they are taken from booklets put out in the 1960s by a firm of shipbuilders. They relate to the crew accommodation on two tankers and a dry cargo ship. The days of the smelly, overcrowded, under-lit, and cramped forecastle, are, thank goodness, over. Indeed, on some vessels (tankers especially) a swimming pool is provided.

A very fair reflection of the modern seaman's lot is provided by this account, from a house magazine, of how the crew of a modern cargo ship (the Blue Star's *Fremantle Star*) planned to spend Christmas at sea in 1960. "As on all ships," the article said, "Christmas can only make limited concessions to the crew. There cannot, and will not, be any let-up on watch keeping duties. But there will be a Christmas tree: there will also be some very jolly decorations, and a magnificent Christmas dinner. We have been given a glimpse of the menu, and we can report that it includes

The P & O cruise liner *Canberra*. Flying has reduced the importance of shipping as a means of long-distance passenger transport, and so the big passenger liners are now mostly used for recreation as cruise ships.

The P & O's *Remuera (right)*, the world's largest refrigerated container ship, is 252 m (827 ft) long and carries 1,151 refrigerated and 300 general purpose 20 foot containers. The crew have private cabins – a contrast to the cramped conditions of even a century ago.

H.M.S. *Bristol*, one of the Royal Navy's guided missile destroyers. The crew's accommodation is as up-to-date as the technical systems on board ship.

iced melon, fried sole, turkey, cold buffet and, of course, Christmas pudding.

"At about eleven o'clock on the morning of Christmas Day, the master, the chief officer, and the chief engineer will visit the sailors' and greasers' messes – to make sure that the festive preparations are well in hand.

"During the afternoon, there will be an organized games tournament and the swimming pool will become a popular place. But the big event of the day takes place at 6.30 p.m., when the Christmas dinner is served. To make the occasion more informal, all attempts at normal seating arrangements are abandoned, and there are balloons, crackers, and all the traditional fun. At the end of the meal, toasts will be drunk to wives and sweethearts and other loved ones at home.

"It is now the turn of the officers to take over the stewards' jackets and serve them their Christmas dinner. Afterwards, there will be a sing-song and a shipboard race meeting." The *Fremantle Star* was scheduled to round Cape Leeuwin on the south-west corner of Australia while all this was taking place.

By no means all sailors enjoyed such comforts. Nevertheless, when the standard at the top rises, the lower end of the scale is hoisted above the mass of mediocrity. The days of small combines, with all their savings invested in a single ship and finding it hard to make ends meet, are long past. The shipping business, like the rest of industry, has been subjected to mergers and take-overs. With larger owners has come greater wealth – and, with it, improved conditions. Nobody, any longer, goes hungry at sea – on Christmas or any other day.

The sailor of old times used to pass his spare time at sea – notably during the "dog watches" between four and six p.m. and six and eight p.m., which were the recognized periods for relaxation – working at various hobbies. Some made models of their vessels (the more ambitious erected them in bottles); some devoted themselves to the execution of primitive paintings; and so on. But it would be a mistake to imagine that all these men were good at arts and crafts – just as the illusion persists that every French prisoner in the Napoleonic Wars had a genius for making model ships out of human bones. Many of them were bored: some were too weary to do anything but sleep.

Nowadays, the crew finds its recreation playing table tennis: there are regular film shows on a number of ships, and, in the better fitted-out coastal vessels, there is always the television. Standards, of course, vary a good deal; but, by and large, they are high.

Perhaps the last link with the past was cut by the Royal Navy in 1970, when the daily rum ration was abolished. The money saved was distributed to naval charities and other organizations catering for the seamen's welfare. Instead of his daily issue of grog, the sailor receives an extra can of beer. With no flogging to watch, presumably, the men do not require such strong liquor.

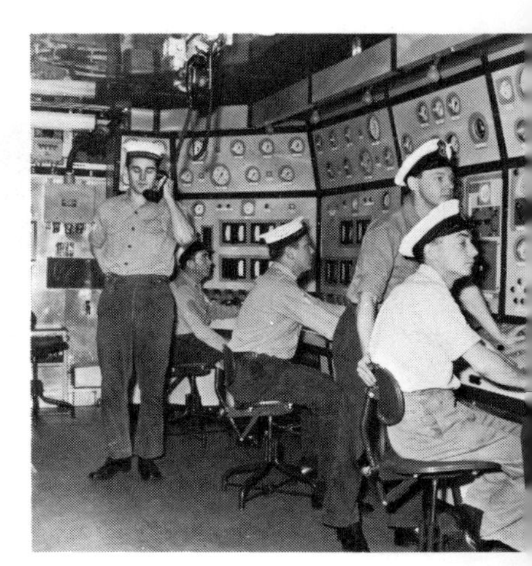

The machinery control room on board H.M.S. *Devonshire*, one of Britain's anti-missile ships. The crew have to be highly skilled technicians to handle the sophisticated machinery – a far cry from the days when few sailors could even read a compass.

Lunchtime for the ratings on board H.M.S. *Juno*. The accommodation, food, pay and leisure time enjoyed by today's sailors would make the service almost unrecognizable for seamen of previous years.

APPENDIX: THE CHANGING STYLE OF SHIPS

c1066, William the Conqueror's longship *Mora*

15th century single-masted ship

16th century, Drake's *Golden Hind*, formerly *Pelican*

1637, *Sovereign of the Seas*, the largest warship in Pepys's navy

1765, Nelson's flagship *Victory*

1837, *Seringapatam*, an East Indiaman

1869, the famous clipper ship, *Cutty Sark*

1802, *Charlotte Dundas*, the first practical steamboat

1840, *Britannia*, the first Cunarder

1911, *Olympic*, a transatlantic giant

1906, *Dreadnought*, the first modern battleship

1960, the guided missile destroyer *Devonshire*

1970, supertanker *British Explorer*

TIME CHART

1194 Richard I returns from Third Crusade: confirms the Laws of Oléron (a charter for seamen), and introduces Mediterranean ideas into English shipbuilding.
1277 Cinque Ports established by Edward I to provide the sovereign with the nucleus of a navy in time of war.
1340 Battle of Sluys: first clash of arms in The Hundred Years' War, and the definitive early type of sea battle.
1410 *Christopher of the Tower* becomes first English ship to be armed with guns.
1488 Bartholomew Diaz rounds the Cape of Good Hope.
1492 Christopher Columbus discovers Cuba and Haiti.
1497 John Cabot sails from Bristol and discovers Newfoundland.
1520 Ferdinand Magellan discovers channel linking South Atlantic and South Pacific. One of his captains makes first circumnavigation of world; but Magellan is killed in the Philippines in 1521.
1577 Francis Drake demolishes the myth of Terra Incognita: discovers Cape Horn, and makes second circumnavigation of world.
1588 Spanish Armada defeated.
1600 Sir James Lancaster discovers that lemon juice, taken regularly, is a preventative for scurvy.
East India Company granted Royal Charter.
1609 East India Company builds *Trade's Increase*, the first British merchantman of over 1,000 tons.
1651 Navigation Act passed, forbidding import of goods to England unless they are carried in English ships – or in vessels belonging to country in which the goods were produced. A similar act had been passed by Richard II, but was unenforceable due to insufficient English shipping.
1660 Pepys enters Navy Office. Introduces reforms to Navy which, eventually, lead to the establishment of a "professional naval officer."
1823 Navigation Act repealed.
1835 Seamen's Registration Act passed – makes it illegal for anyone to be "detained against his consent in the Navy Service of His Majesty for a longer period than five years" unless he had volunteered for a longer period.
1850 "An Act for improving the conditions of Masters, Mates and Seamen, and maintaining discipline in the Merchant Service" empowers the Board of Trade to inspect ships and introduces compulsory exams for officers.
1857 Naval Ratings given an official uniform.
1859 Royal Naval Reserve founded.
1869 Clipper ship *Sir Lancelot* makes passage from Foochow to London in 89 days – an all-time record for sail in the tea trade.

Clipper ship *Thermopylae* sails from London to Melbourne in sixty days on her maiden voyage: establishes an all-time record for sail on the passage to Australia.

Suez Canal opened by Empress Eugenie of France – cutting the distance from London to Bombay by 4,500 nautical miles.

1871 Flogging in the Navy "suspended in peacetime."

1876 Plimsoll mark established, making the overloading of ships illegal.

1879 Flogging in the Navy "suspended in wartime."

1880 Merchant Seamen (Payment of wages and Rating) Act abolishes "advance notes," thereby ending the ability of crimps to rob seamen of wages not yet due to them. This act also ruled that a merchant seaman should be entitled to the rating of AB after he had served at sea for four years before the mast.

1887 National Amalgamated Sailors and Firemen's Union of Great Britain and Ireland founded.

1903 Royal Naval Volunteer Reserve founded.

1909 Cooks' and Stewards' Union founded.

1914–18 First World War.

1915 Panama Canal opened, shortening distance by sea from London to San Francisco by 5,500 miles.

1926 Name of seamen's union changed to National Union of Seamen. The union refuses to take part in the General Strike.

1932 Shipping depression at its worst: 40,000 seamen out of work – 1,663,000 tons of British shipping laid up.

1939–45 World War II.

1940 Merchant Navy Reserve Pool established, giving seamen the opportunity of continuous employment.

1960 Seamen given a 5½-day week (44-hour week in port) and a 7½ per cent. pay rise.

1972 Navy abolishes daily issue of rum.

LIST OF READING

Adam W. Kirkaldy, *British Shipping*, 1914; David & Charles, 1970.
Stan Hugill, *Sailor Town*, Routledge, 1967.
Geoffrey Penn, *Up Funnel, Down Screw!*, Hollis & Carter, 1955.
Oliver Warner, *The Navy*, Penguin, 1968.
William Hickey, *Memoirs: 1782–90*, Hutchinson, 1923.
L. P. Kirwan, *A History of Polar Exploration*, Hollis & Carter, 1959.
John Masefield, *Sea Life in Nelson's Time*, 1905; Conway Maritime Press, 1971.
Richard Hough, *The Blind Horn's Hate*, Hutchinson, 1971.
William Robinson, *Jack Nastyface*, 1836; Wayland, 1973.
Roger Hart, *England Expects*, Wayland, 1972.
Christopher Lloyd, *The British Seaman*, 1968; Paladin, 1970.
W. E. Home, *Merchant Seamen*, Murray, 1922.
E. S. Turner, *Gallant Gentlemen – a portrait of the British Officer, 1600–1956*, Michael Joseph, 1956.
J. Lennox Kerr and Wilfred Granville, *The R.N.V.R.*, Harrap, 1957.
Peter Kemp, *The British Sailor*, Dent, 1971.
Sir Walter Runciman, *Collier Brigs and their Sailors*, 1926; Conway Maritime Press, 1971.
The Story of the Seamen – a short history of the National Union of Seamen, National Union of Seamen, 1964.
Stan Hugill, *Shanties from the Seven Seas*, Routledge, 1961.

Acknowledgements

The publishers thank the following for loaning pictures used to illustrate this book: The Trustees of the National Maritime Museum, frontispiece, pp. 21 bottom, 32, 34, 37, 42, 45, 48, 50, 57–9, 62, 63 top, 64–5, 66, 68, 73, 78–9, 81 top, 84, 91, 109 bottom left and right, 117 top, colour section: second, third and fourth pages; The Trustees of the British Museum, pp. 6, 33, colour section, first page; The Trustees of the National Portrait Gallery, pp. 7, 9 top, 13, 31; The Mansell Collection, pp. 8 left, 10, 18, 20 right, 28–9, 55, 60–1, 71, 72 bottom, 81 bottom, 90, 94–6, 106 bottom, 113 top, 115–16; Mary Evans Picture Library, pp. 9 bottom, 11 top, 14 bottom, 16, 17 top, 53 bottom, 69–70, 72 top, 75–6, 80, 82–3, 88, 91 top, 104–5, 111; Radio Times Hulton Picture Library, pp. 12 bottom, 40 left, 51, 54; P. & O. Lines Ltd., pp. 74, 117 bottom, 118 top; Brunel University Library, p. 92; Kodak Ltd., pp. 101, 110, 113 bottom; The Trustees of the Imperial War Museum, p. 106 top; Ministry of Defence, pp. 118, 119 bottom; Keystone Press Agency Ltd., p. 119 top. The ships illustrated in the Appendix were drawn by Tony Garrett.

Index